CW01652993

From gambler to entrepreneur

From Gambling to Success Strategy

PRIAN IPAT

Copyright © 2024 Ciprian Ipate

All rights reserved. No part of this book may be reproduced, stored in a retrieval system, or transmitted in any form or by any means, whether electronic, mechanical, photocopying, recording, or otherwise, without the express written permission of the publisher and author.

ISBN: 979-88-9170-087-1

Publicat de: Bookllo Publishing

ABOUT THE AUTHOR

We shared hard-learned lessons and personal experiences in the book "From Player to Entrepreneur." I have made difficult decisions to change my life instead of choosing easy choices for the hard life that awaits me. How did I get involved in gambling? What are the factors that have affected my life? How did we overcome these challenges? Now, I have made a promise to myself that I will help others by sharing my experiences and tips with readers so they can escape the curse of gambling addiction and also for a brighter future.

This book is dedicated to those who struggle with gambling addiction.

It is for those who are exhausted by their gaming habits and who want to break this vicious circle.

Table of Contents

Introduction: From player to entrepreneur

This book was written with the aim of highlighting the dark side of gambling addiction and how it can destroy lives. I see it as a personal mission to be a support for those struggling with this problem and to initiate a movement against this devastating addiction.

Gambling addiction is a severely underestimated and often misunderstood problem. My goal with this book is to change this perspective and realize the importance of deeply understanding this addiction. I committed to sharing everything: my tumultuous journey, lessons learned and mistakes made, all with an open heart and honesty. I hope this will inspire and offer hope to those struggling with this difficult issue, guiding them towards a path of transformation.

This book is not just a text, but a guide that will accompany you through the maze of gambling addiction and give you a clear plan to success. My book is divided into three parts.

The first part presents my own story about gambling addiction, starting with my first experience with bookmakers and the exciting atmosphere of gambling, describing the picture of temptation that finally caught me. After numerous struggles along this journey, navigating the heights and depths of addiction, I was finally able to regain control of my life.

Part two of my book focuses on ways to prevent gambling addiction and even overcome it. Here you will find actionable steps and tested methods to quit addiction and keep you on track. It is important to understand that giving up and maintaining abstinence is an ongoing process, requiring long-term commitment.

Finally, part three reflects the complete transformation from gamblers into successful entrepreneurs. Here, you'll find guidance and tips on how to thrive in life. Sales can build a successful career and improve personal relationships.

This book gives you the tools to overcome your gambling addiction, rediscover yourself, and create a fulfilling and successful life. The path to this transformation can bring challenges, but together, we can face anything and move towards a more enlightened and satisfying life.

My little wish? I hope that these words will be able to change at least one person's life. Of course, I dream of a bigger impact, but to make a positive change to at least one life would be like a jackpot for me. Let's be honest, we're not born with gambling addiction in our DNA any more than we're born alcoholics or substance users. It is the influence of the world around us, publicity and social pressures that can influence us.

This promise is about fighting gambling addiction, ending this vicious cycle and starting a new era. Through this book, I hope that by sharing my own learning journey and methods of quitting gambling, I can make a positive difference in the lives of others.

So this is just the beginning of the adventure I offer in this book. I hope my story and commitment to this fight will inspire as many people as possible, guiding them to a more prosperous and fulfilling life.

"You'll never succeed if you don't start. But once you start, you'll never be the same." – Zig Ziglar

Part 1: Promise

Buckle up for the first part, in which I will share with you my experiences and mistakes. There is no judgment here; I simply expose them. I hope my stories will give you real insight and an edge in understanding the gambling addiction network.
A bright hope for a life without gambling. Looking back at the pain caused by gambling and reinforcing your commitment to breaking free from the vicious circle, emphasizing that quitting gambling is not a one-time decision, but an ongoing process. Sharing this rollercoaster ride is expected to be a guiding light for others going through similar storms.
Be careful: it's not just about gamblers. Families, friends and neighbors are all caught in the crossfire. This book isn't just about problems. It is a toolkit for solutions. Together, we will kick this curse and paint the picture of a healthier and more balanced life. Let us walk this path together, with the hope that my words will shake and inspire those who fight against this brutal addiction. Let's be honest, it's not easy at all. But we can master it and gain some control. And yes, I have a backpack full of my own mistakes and failures that I throw at you so you can avoid them.
The sad truth is that many people begin to experience these sins when they take their first steps into adulthood, tasting freedom and trying to decipher life's responsibilities.

This promise is not just a promise; It is a vibration, a guiding light for anyone who is entangled in the shadows of addiction. It is a testimony to the belief that together we are stronger and that overcoming gambling addiction is not a job for one person. It's a group effort.
In this book, I will tell you that there is always hope of recovery from any challenge, be it gambling or not.
Yes, I gambled. Now, the reason I started gambling is because I started playing with the negative effects of my social circle. It took me an impossibly long time to realize I had a problem and find a way out.
In the past, people around me influenced me and I got involved without realizing the dangers that awaited me. How deeply I was

absorbed. It is a discouraging and bittersweet feeling that you are now trapped in an evil from which you cannot escape. Recognizing the problem was a crucial and challenging moment for me. I had to accept that I had an addiction and that I had to control it. Despite my misunderstandings, I need to take serious steps to achieve this.
The main idea is to introduce you to my world, giving you a deep perspective so that you can learn to organise your own activities more effectively. By sharing my experiences, I open the book of my life so that you can draw valuable lessons from my errors. We're all travelers on this tumultuous adventure called life, right? If I manage to make you understand this innovation, I feel that I have gained enormously.
Even though it seems complicated and sometimes impossible to avoid this evil, I assure you that with determined confidence, we can find ways to take control and recover in order to recover our lives and live a whole of contentment.
It's like shouting on the rooftop, "I'm here to stay and I care." It's not just a personal discussion; It is a joint effort to face the challenges that come with the enticing claws of gambling, fully aware that they can turn lives upside down.
This promise is not a solitary mission. It's a statement to stay standing against the odds. It's an outstretched hand to those stuck in the sticky nets of addiction, saying, "I'll cover you."

Imagine this promise as a journey of understanding and recovery. The person who makes the promise to help others is like a beacon, guiding others through the stormy seas of addiction. It's not just about personal power; It's about having an entire community ready to throw a lifeline.
Taking on a gambling addiction is more than just words. It's a vow to break the cycle of bad choices. It's about changing destructive habits with a fresh start, a commitment to healing and rebuilding. It's like saying, "Compassion, understanding, and a spine of steel. We will turn this ship around."

My story

Making a decisive decision at 16, after completing the school year, I started working in a bakery. Coming from a family with limited financial possibilities, this step represented my entry into the adult world. It was an experience that attracted me enormously, giving me the opportunity to earn my own money. This opportunity instilled in me a deep desire and an unwavering determination to succeed. I felt I was gaining financial independence and strength, and I was determined to achieve more.

Every day, I passionately learned every step of bread making, from preparing the dough to removing the bread from the oven and placing it in crates. I enjoyed every moment I turned simple ingredients into a satisfying final product. Over time, my bosses began to appreciate me for my bread-making skills.

When I look back, I wonder if it was a decent decision. I chose to drop out of school to earn a monthly income and advance my career. I decided to leave school because of my desire to grow up. I tried to be the best at my job, but upbringing and education were just as important.

This skill taught me that success is not only measured in money and positions, but it is essential to find a balance between our desire to win and the realization of our true passions and ideals. We should remember to take charge of personal development and fully enjoy life.

Today, as I write this book, I understand that it is essential to be the best at what we do, but it is equally important to listen to our feelings and be consistently excellent.

> "True wisdom comes from recognizing that education is a lifelong process and that our personal development never stops." – John Dewey

At the age of 17, I started getting involved in the world of gambling. I was dating older boys in a neighborhood in Romania,

where people lived without big dreams; In a way, it was neighborhood life.
During a discussion with a friend, I discovered a job opportunity as a salesman in a certain place, Constanta, by the sea, and the idea of working in such an attractive environment, with beautiful girls on the beach and parties, immediately attracted me. I didn't hesitate to say it was an opportunity I couldn't miss.
I was excited that day. My friend had spoken to me only the day before, but my resolve was so firm that I felt no hesitation in acting. I went home and told my mom about my decision to go to the beach, but she initially thought I was joking. In the evening I tried to tell her that I would leave tomorrow, but for her it was something she couldn't believe. I woke up early on the morning of my departure when my mother expressed concern. It's hard to accept that sometimes our decisions affect our loved ones, but my decision was firm then. I knew I had to follow this path. When he saw that I woke up in the morning and I wasn't joking, he started talking to me and thinking again, because when I had something in my head to do, it was hard to change my mind. After several discussions, she started crying and brought me some clothes and a towel to take with me. And he made me some sandwiches, just like in school.
In addition to the excitement and determination to go ashore during this time, I also had a concern about my six-year-old younger sister and did not fully realize at the time that I was influencing her. And I was going to be away from her at such a critical time for her development. I was wondering if I would attend the sea or how this decision would affect our relationship. It was a challenge to associate my dream with my desire.
Although it was difficult to take an unknown step away from my daily routine, I am grateful for the courage to accept this opportunity to earn my own money and be responsible for my journey, which gave me freedom. I really felt like an adult. Although this decision came with challenges and uncertainties, it was a time full of enthusiasm and opportunities for personal development and interaction with people from different backgrounds. It helped me understand myself better and discover my passion for sales and interacting with people. I can't describe the difficult times I went through, but I also admit that this adventure taught me many valuable lessons. I learned to

take risks, follow my passion and create a story. Not everything was perfect, but I grew up and learned a lot about myself and life.

"Life is where your comfort zone ends," Neale Donald Walsch said.

At work, I had the opportunity to meet a member of the team who introduced me to the world of gambling, in a different way than I had learned in the neighborhood, especially with the slot game, which played an important role in my evolution in the field of gambling. He was a man full of life and enthusiasm, always ready to explore and experiment. With each day we spent together, we began to share the same passion for adrenaline and excitement that these games offered. My partner fascinated me with stories about impressive winnings and the intensity of emotions he felt in the presence of slot machines. He was passionately telling me about those moments when the reels were spinning madly, giving rise to victorious combinations on screen. These stories fueled my curiosity about those capable of generating such powerful feelings, and the desire to be around them became more intense day by day.

So, one day, we decided to go together to a huge casino to try the slots. It was a vibrant and lively place, where the distinctive sounds of slot machines and the enthusiastic voices of players resounded. Looking around, I felt like an explorer in a new universe, ready to discover the secrets of these games. In front of me lay rows of slots, each with unique themes and features that appealed to different people. I carefully selected a slot machine to try out the big options and prizes, put money into it and couldn't wait to start my journey into the world of gambling.

As the symbols lined up on the screen, I felt a wave of emotions engulf me. Every moment was a mixture of excitement and suspense; Even a short win brought immense joy. I was losing track of time in front of the machine, hoping for that perfect combination and trusting that luck was on my side. I didn't know that gambling is a bit like a cunning trick. They trick you into thinking it's easy to win, but reality often brings negative consequences, and the thrill of winning is quickly followed by disappointment. In my youthful naivety about gambling, I fell into

the trap of believing that quick and easy winnings can last forever. Without knowing it, I became addicted to gambling.
It is essential to understand that, despite occasional gains and some successes, relying solely on luck and youth is not a sustainable plan. The perks may seem tempting, but they can wreak havoc on your life, affecting relationships, finances, and emotions.
My journey into the world of gambling marked a turning point, pushing me to face my weaknesses and regain control of my life. Winning a few times fueled my excitement, but I knew it wasn't a path to continue. The new lifestyle brought a sense of freedom and adventure, especially the excitement and adrenaline that captivated me.

However, the danger of this obsession with gambling began to grip me. Instead of focusing on education and building a future, I got lost in the game, constantly looking for more gains. It took me a while to realize that I had jeopardized my future and lost myself. This addiction caused problems in my relationships and mental health and pushed me to a point where I could no longer ignore the problems. It took serious steps to regain control.
Imagine what I could have done with the money I spent on gambling, getting a driver's license, investing in education, saving for a house, traveling and discovering the world. Our lives teach us to listen to our parents or teachers, but we lack sufficient guidance on money management and wise financial decisions.
This is my perspective, and others may have different experiences with financial education. In my case, the lack of proper education left me vulnerable. I therefore stress the importance of financial education and maintaining a healthy balance between entertainment and finance. Despite my mistakes, I hope my story serves as a warning and encourages others facing a similar struggle to make wise decisions about money and life.
In the years that followed, I dedicated myself to hard work and excellence. Every day, I strived to learn and hone my skills, aiming to be the best on my team. Success quickly came to work, but every night I got lost in the maze of casinos. Small gambling halls were no longer enough; I looked for bigger casinos, where temptation and danger lurked. Gambling has hindered my

personal and professional development, despite traveling and meeting new people.
Chronic fatigue caused by sleepless nights in casinos affected my work, preventing me from focusing on projects. Losing money for rent has become increasingly common, which has increased financial pressure. I spent sleepless and adventurous nights with my boyfriend, often without money for accommodation. I vividly remember an extremely cold winter night when we could not afford to pay for a hotel. The train station became our shelter, with radiators providing warmth on that freezing night. It was one of the worst nights I've had. We spent all our money that day at the casino and couldn't pay for the hotel afterwards. Away from home, without anyone knowing.
We had argued over who would sleep first and for how long. A train controller came because he had heard a noise at one point and wanted to kick us out. That was the last thing I needed. Even though it was one of the worst nights I've had, now I smile when I think of her. And it wasn't the only misfortune or punishment for our actions. With the same friend, after losing all the money at the casino, we had to return to another city where we already had accommodation. But with no money, we hitchhiked to find a car to head to the city we were supposed to reach. And, unfortunately, it was winter again. When we left, the morning was sunny and pleasant, but in the evening there was a terrible blizzard. He was wearing a thin jacket, while I had a thicker one. It was so cold that he started crying and we decided that until we could get out of there, we would exchange jackets so that he could warm up a little.

In the following periods, forced to face financial shortages, we ended up sleeping on park benches. People say hardship is part of the road to success, but I realized I was self-destructive through my obsession with gambling. Those difficult nights were the result of addiction, jeopardizing stability and well-being.

Time passes relentlessly, leaving no opportunity to back down.

My birthdays are not occasions I look forward to. They often bring a sense of sadness, seeming to be the loneliest day of the year. Why celebrate the passing of another year? What have I really accomplished by simply adding another year to my life?
Instead, I find more value in the other 364 days—times for reflection and faithful planning. My birthday becomes a time of introspection rather than celebration, a time to meditate on the passage of time and the changes in my life.
My birthdays varied dramatically, influenced by circumstances and the people around me. Some were just days of contemplation, a chance to think about the time that has passed and my choices. You can't make up for time spent or undo past mistakes, but you can learn and grow from them.
Despite this birthday, I console myself in moments of real change, such as New Year's Eve and Christmas, when hope and goodness prevail. My birthday may be overshadowed by sadness, but it's encouraging to know that there are times when the world lights up with positivity and creates unforgettable memories.
I feel nervous and frustrated telling you that time slips relentlessly without leaving any opportunity to rewind. It's amazing how much time it takes to build something meaningful or nurture relationships, and how quickly the wrong words can undo them. Regret is an ever-present shadow, and wasted time is irrevocable.
We plan almost every aspect of life, from daily commutes to dream vacations. However, we often neglect to plan life itself. Time slips unnoticed, and it may be too late when we stop to think about it. These missed opportunities and moments remain in our memory.
This is especially true for habits such as smoking or gambling. We make excuses to keep going until something drastic prompts us to act. But why wait for a crisis? Why not choose proactive change today? What's stopping you?

A new chapter in my life

At some point, I recognized the need for radical change. I boldly abandoned that lifestyle, redirecting my ambition and resources to a higher purpose. By a determined decision, I decided to open my own company, an essential step in my journey towards recovery and reconstruction. At that time, despite my young age, I had the ability and skills to be more constructive and beneficial to myself and others.

Opening your own company was an important turning point and an independent decision. Although it was only the beginning of a much more substantial challenge, it gave me the freedom to do what I wanted and earn even more. However, gambling has had a profound effect on my life. Whether I was always in the same place every night or how much money I wasted in front of gambling machines, I can say that I am a good person. I've been through many doors and I'm not proud, but now I realize my mistakes.

Gambling has had a devastating effect on my life, taking me away from the things that matter and causing me to lose relationships and passions more than I can bear. Looking back, I admit that I made serious mistakes in managing money and priorities. I found satisfaction and excitement in gambling, but I ignored the long-term consequences. I lost confidence in myself and the trust of many people around me, not to mention precious time.

This business revolved around computers and phones. As these devices became increasingly popular, a second-hand sales market emerged. Many young people bought phones online and resold them for profit, an adventure I embarked on. However, the small gains from buying and selling a few phones were not satisfactory.

Investing all my money in slot machines constantly left me broke, which forced me to start a legitimate, fully equipped business. Despite this, I decided to open a small store for buying and selling phones. Before, when an idea came to me, I acted immediately, without patience. One evening, I went downtown to research potential locations. Surprisingly, we found a space that had been a GSM service store and was for rent. I grabbed my contact details and planned to call the next morning, convinced I didn't need to look any further. The location was known as a GSM service center, so I expected to have customers from day one.

The next day, I called to inquire about the price and other details, but I didn't have the funds to start a business. The woman who answered provided me with all the necessary information, and the rent seemed affordable. I promised to call again, but the reality of not having funds for rent or starting a business was daunting, not to mention the unforeseen extra expenses. Under pressure, I turned to a friend to borrow some money. Being a player, I knew that even close friends hesitate to lend money to a player. Fortunately, I was able to get the necessary funds to start my adventure.

With no money and no knowledge of phones, I set out to open my store. The real challenge came when I went to inspect the place at night. I hadn't yet considered neighborhood business. The GSM service, which had supposedly shut down, had moved next door. Initially, this caused some panic because friends warned me that I would fail by having a direct competitor so close. However, I chose to look at the situation positively: the location was already known for GSM services, which would naturally attract potential customers. The fact that my store was first in line was an advantage because customers visited mine first.

My original plan was to buy and sell phones, not fix them, which I thought would differentiate my business from neighboring GSM service. I started buying damaged phones to learn how to fix them before reselling them. Gradually, I began to accumulate skills in repairing them. Often customers visited my store first, usually asking about repairs and accessories. The idea of repairing phones was daunting—damaging one's own phones was a problem, but the risk of damaging customers' phones was an even greater responsibility. I tried asking for help from the neighboring GSM store to avoid direct competition and outsource repairs I was hesitant to do myself. However, the relationship was strained; They often refused or delayed repairs.

This situation motivated me to learn more about repairs and start selling accessories on my own. I managed to master phone repair. My store was open from 9 a.m. to 6 p.m., but I often stayed up until midnight, trying to fix as many phones as I could. A fellow repairman on another street became a great help and mentor to me on this learning journey.

The hard work and skills acquired began to pay off. The customer base grew so much that we hired two employees. Having employees allowed me to have more free time, but that wasn't necessarily a good thing. I spent all my free time, and even my working hours, in gambling halls, often with my friends. All my daily earnings were wasted, leaving me without funds for new investments. The potential of my store was enormous, but my gambling habits were gradually undermining it and nullifying all the hard work I had done. Although I enjoyed the knowledge and mastery I had acquired, I let myself be swallowed up again by the world of gambling, just like before.

It is essential to recognize and learn from my mistakes, so I can say that this experience inspired me to take responsibility and find solutions to overcome gambling addiction and build a healthy and balanced life. After my experience in business, I went through a difficult period where I could barely handle the business anymore and I was close to closing it. However, I managed to run it for about a year and a half. I learned many lessons and it was time to learn from my mistakes and take a new direction in life.

I was determined to give up my passion for gambling and build a better life. I realized I had to do this, especially since many were starting to drift away from me. Being aware that society is reluctant to look at those involved in gambling, I set out to find an easier way to make money.

I tried to start a new business, hoping for success and higher income, but, unfortunately, this initiative did not last more than three months. The failure was caused, in part, by the time I spent in casinos, but also by the lack of information and proper training.

In my desperate search for ideas to help me recover, I learned important lessons. To succeed in business or projects, clear vision, broad knowledge and careful planning are essential. I researched and implemented a new idea, but I needed more funds. With courage and confidence in success, I started this new business, developed it, worked hard and dedicated a whole year to it. It wasn't a resounding success, but the potential was huge. However, at some point, I stopped.

For a while, I reduced the frequency of gambling, believing that I was beginning to get rid of this vice. But once I started having money again, I went back to my old habits, spending my earnings recklessly. I noticed how those around me were progressing far beyond my point, which made me feel guilty.

Also, many people do not have a relationship with their parents that allows them to talk openly about their problems, for fear that they will be blamed and criticized for wasting time and spending money on reckless things. Unfortunately, very few parents understand this issue and are willing to offer help and guidance.

You can't live your whole life in fear that someone will reject your decisions or advice, and such fear can isolate you even more.

I have distanced myself from many friends and relatives because who would want to deal with someone who wastes their money and time gambling? We've seen numerous examples, both in movies and in real life, of how gambling addiction has ruined lives. I've had friends who ended up stealing items from their homes to finance gambling. It's heartbreaking to see how far people are willing to go just for a chance to bet.

People often express frustration about lack of job opportunities, feeling neglected by the government, or not feeling understood by friends and family. But behind these complaints, there seems to be a noticeable reluctance to desire self-improvement and learning. It is important to realize that although life can take away from us almost anything—from material possessions like a car and home, to fundamental ties to family, spouse—there is something priceless that no one can take away from us: accumulated knowledge and wisdom.

I used the term "ex-friends" to emphasize the ending of relationships that no longer bring positive value to my life. It is essential to separate ourselves from people who influence us negatively. I have always been open to making new friendships, provided they enrich me – whether they are smarter, giving me the opportunity to learn and evolve, or people with a big heart, able to provide emotional support. Grief and regret often come too late, in moments of bitter reflection when we face significant loss: wasted financial resources, lost true friends, painful separations, and, worst of all, when our family loses trust in us.

Look for documentaries and learn about others who have gone through the same situation; There is a chance to completely stop the addiction. Don't play at all. Many claim they will play less, but I want to tell you the story of another friend, a player. He states that he is not a compulsive gambler and can limit himself to playing only once or twice a year. But when he plays, he loses all the money in his pocket, bets large amounts, equivalent to average monthly salaries. Can it be said that it is limited?

We are poor or rich depending on who we compare ourselves to. If we look at someone richer than us, we will indeed feel inferior, but if we look at someone much poorer, we will undoubtedly feel rich. Don't feel alone in this struggle. You might need help. You may encounter obstacles, but with the right support and perseverance, you can find your way to a more balanced and healthy life.

I've been through the same things and frustrations. I did and intended to quit gambling, but it only had a temporary effect. In the end, I fell into the same trap. The emphasis is on doing as much as possible and ignoring negative consequences.

When it comes to gambling, your mind is divided. Voices are fighting inside you. A voice promises big wins and instant gratification. It encourages you to bet more. This voice tells you that you will be lucky. It gives you and deceives you with fake materials of wealth and success.

However, another voice, the voice of reason, tells you that gambling is a mistake, that you risk losing more than you gain, and that it reminds you of the disastrous financial consequences, the destruction of personal relationships, and the loss of emotional stability. It is less noisy, but is often overlooked by the desire to bet and the excitement of the moment.

In the heart of Romania lies Targu Jiu, a city as beautiful as it is serene, with its charming river and the tranquility of its parks. But one evening, in this picturesque setting, I learned a lesson far from the tranquility of its landscapes.

After a day of work, a friend and I found ourselves drawn to the flickering neon lights of a casino and decided to go in with a casual shrug as a thought of our day. We were harmless emotion seekers, or so we told ourselves. However, as the hours passed, our gambling became more than just a pastime. They turned into a living show of hope and despair, victories and losses intertwined like threads of destiny.

The clocks moved unnoticed, running towards midnight as we continued playing. In that casino, time and responsibility seemed to dissolve, leaving only the thrill of the game. It was a thrill that cost us everything we had in our pockets, a price we only fully understood when we returned to reality. The cold night air of Targu Jiu greeted us, a cruel reminder of what we had lost.

Realization dawned upon us, cruel and unforgiving. We had no money left for our stay, no funds for food, not even enough for the humble comfort of a coffee. The charm of the casino turned into a harsh awakening, leaving us with empty wallets and a sense of regret.

Having no other refuge, we found solace in the city park, which quietly judges our choices. Walking along the Jiu River, the serene environment contrasted sharply with the chaos we had just left behind. We made promises to each other, vows that this would be our last gamble. But such promises, made in the shadow of loss, often sound like emptiness. The words echoed countless times I had heard similar resolutions from others, each time followed by a return to the same old patterns.

That night, under the open sky in Targu Jiu, I slept on a park bench, not for the first time and certainly not for the last. It was a night of inconvenient truths, an achievement that quickly freed me from the grip of gambling is no easy task. People often say that quitting gambling is simply a matter of willpower; You just stop and you're done. But that night taught me the intricacies of

addiction; It's not like a switch we can flip, but a journey, often with painful steps.
When dawn came, painting the sky in shades of hope, I lay on the bench, meditating. It was a moment of clarity in the midst of a life mired in confusion and inappropriate desires.

The lesson from Targu Jiu was clear: the path of gambling is deceptive, full of more than financial pitfalls – it is a path that tests your sense of self and control. This awareness was a small but crucial step on my long road from the clutches of gambling to the freedom and challenges of entrepreneurship.
I had moved to another city. This city was a novelty to me, a different scene in the familiar play of my playing life. As soon as I arrived, I felt drawn to a gambling establishment as an invisible force. The first day there promised something extraordinary.
I sat down at a slot machine, the familiar buzz and flashing lights being a comforting backdrop for my anticipation. Nearby, luck smiled broadly at a fellow player who won a jackpot so big it seemed to electrify the air. In an unexpected gesture of generosity, he began sharing his winnings with others in the venue in a celebration of his good fortune. It seemed that luck had a contagious quality, and I found myself the beneficiary of his generosity.
With this unexpected gift in hand, I played. Gains and losses danced together as the hours went by, fading into their rhythm. Towards evening, I left the place with my pockets unusually full, the weight of money being a tangible reminder of the success of the day.
But success, in the world of gambling, is a siren song. The win on day one was a beacon that drew me back, not just the next day, but for two whole weeks. Like a moth on the flame, I was there from morning to night, more dedicated to these machines than to any real job. The venue became my world, where time, hunger, and even basic needs became irrelevant.
Inside that dimly lit space, I was as much a fixed element as cars; The need to keep playing eclipsed everything else. Even the most basic human needs—to eat and get some fresh air—seemed like unwanted distractions. In those days, you could

smoke indoors, so, armed with cigarettes and an endless supply of coffee, I stuck to my chair.
This relentless routine transformed me. Every day, I felt more like a zombie, physically present but lost to the outside world. From morning till late at night, the gambling cycle consumed me. And, as is often the case, the initial series of luck was a deceptive prelude to the inevitable.
Despite occasional gains, the relentless appeal of the machines meant that all the money I earned was quickly reabsorbed, along with much more from my pocket. The harsh reality of gambling is this: even when luck favors you, the house always has an advantage. Spurred on by the elusive promise of the big win, players often end up betting back their winnings and more.
As the two weeks approached, I walked out of the room not as a winner, but as a man drained of more than money. My pockets were empty and my spirit exhausted. This experience, in a city like any other, was a harsh lesson about the deceptive nature of gambling. It's not just about lost money, it's also about time and self-sacrifice on the altar of the game.

In the world of gamblers, attraction isn't always about the promise of wealth; Sometimes it's the seductive atmosphere that captivates you, an atmosphere often amplified by the presence of fascinating women. Let's now explore another incident in another city.

When I went inside, it was clear that the whispers were not exaggerated. The venue was a picture of elegance and allure, each table being hosted by women whose beauty was matched only by their performance. They were the mermaids of this modern story from The Odyssey, their charm being a subtle but powerful attraction to the enchanted clientele who gathered at tables. A roulette table hosted by a woman whose smile was as captivating as the spinning of the wheel. Her presence was an ingenious mixture of sophistication and warmth, which made gambling seem more like a dance. The conversations were easy, but her laughter also made the losses less bitter. This place wasn't just a place to bet; It was a land where beauty and chance intertwined, creating an intoxicating atmosphere that made you want to stay, play and be part of this enchanting world. Every smile and graceful gesture of the hosts added to the charm, making the risk of the bet seem even more appealing.

But as night progressed, the façade slowly faded. It was realized that beauty and charm were as much a part of the game as cards and chips. The attraction was a strategic masterpiece, a call of mermaids that drew you even more into the game. It was a powerful cocktail of desire and hope mixed with the thrill of the game.

I left the place late at night, my pockets lighter than when I entered. As I stepped out into the cold night air, I couldn't help but reflect on the evening. It was a lesson about the many faces of gambling, a world where admired beauty is woven into the fabric of temptation. This experience taught me that in gambling, the charm extends beyond the promise of money. It's a world where every aspect is carefully curated to keep you at the table and make you play. Beauty, charm and ambience are all threads in the player's upholstery, each of which pulls you back repeatedly.

In the world of gambling, there is a unique kind of brotherhood, a tacit kinship that binds those who share this vice. It is a bond that transcends the usual barriers of not knowing. This story begins on a day when I met another player, a meeting that turned into hours of stories and shared experiences.

I was in a café, a small, undefined place away from the glare and noise of casinos. There, I met a stranger at first, but a fellow traveler on the path of gambling. The admission was almost immediate, like a silent nod of a shared secret. He, like me, bore the subtle signs of a gambler: anxious eyes, tired but hopeful expression, a certain patience born of long hours of waiting for luck to return.

When we started a conversation, the topics flowed effortlessly. There was no need for formal introductions or small talk. We plunged directly into the heart of our common passion. We talked about the biggest wins, losses, narrow failures and what ifs. Each story is mirrored in the other, reflecting the same patterns of emotion, regret and the relentless pursuit of the great elusive victory.

Our conversation addressed the different facets of gambling. We discussed strategies and superstitions, the charm of the jackpot, the deceptive simplicity of games, and the complex psychology behind each bet. It was a dialogue rich in understanding and empathy, something rare and precious in a world often shrouded in judgments and misconceptions.

Hours passed us as we shared stories of temptation, moments when the thrill of gambling transcended reason and the silent despair that often followed a loss. We talked about the special camaraderie in casinos and the tacit understanding between those who sat at tables or in front of the machines.

But our conversation was not only an exchange of stories, but also a reflection on our journey through gambling. There was a sense of relief in this sharing, feeling understood without explanation. We delved into the reasons that drew us into this world and our challenges in navigating it.

As the evening ended, we parted, we would probably never meet again. But that meeting left a lasting impression. He emphasized the strong bond that gambling can create between people. It reminded us that in the world of gambling, you're never really alone. There are always others who share your experiences, struggles and dreams.

This chance encounter was a testimony to the fact that gambling, with all the ills it has, creates a kind of community – a group of individuals bound by a common journey, each looking for something beyond turning a card or spinning a wheel.

Coming to the UK

After almost a decade of losing money in the world of gambling, I realized that I could no longer continue to walk this self-destructive path and felt the need for significant change.

I decided to leave everything behind and change my lifestyle. So I set my sights on the UK in search of a fresh start and a friendlier environment to rebuild my life. A change of scenery and culture could be the relaunch I needed, not only for stability, but also to regain my confidence and lost purpose.

Moving to the UK was like plunging into the unknown. The uncertainty and challenges of adapting to a new environment, dealing with a foreign language and building a whole new network of relationships became my daily routine. I found a job to live on and started piecing together the financial puzzle.

Every day in the UK was a school day, full of life lessons and chances for personal development. We've learned that we can pull ourselves out of the pits with courage, change, and the right steps to transform our lives. By focusing on personal development, forging better relationships, and finding fulfillment in my work, I was able to live a happier and more balanced life.

But let's be honest, this new chapter wasn't a walk in the park. Quitting gambling was not a breeze; It was an ongoing struggle with the desire to bet. Escaping the vicious circle meant listening to that nagging voice of reason, recognizing the pitfalls of gambling, and understanding that it was just a one-way ticket to misery and loss. It was time to face the music and accept reality. Self-deception and stubborn refusal to see the truth kept me in that hamster wheel.

To overcome addiction, I had to be honest with myself and admit that gambling only brought me trouble and suffering. It meant opening my eyes to the fact that I wasn't invincible and that the odds were against me. Dreams of winning were a mirage, closing my eyes to reality. It took time, dedication, and seeking information from those who had struggled with the same demons. The journey was not smooth; It was a rollercoaster of emotions and uncontrolled temptations. Quitting gambling was a test, a bold choice to take control of my life and weave a happy and

healthy future. Beware of the pitfalls of self-deception and embrace a recovery process where responsibility and self-love are essential.
A solid determination to quit gambling was the anchor that kept me in balance. Surrounding myself with an environment that rooted my fight against gambling, moving away from the places and people that pushed me to return to the game, and finding alternative activities and passions were essential.
We can also seek help from professionals specialized in the treatment of gambling addiction. Everyone has their own path to recovery and must find the best methods. It is essential to be patient and remember that the healing process can take time, but only if you are determined and have the right support. Together, we can overcome this addiction and regain control of life.
It is essential to understand that the main purpose of casinos and gambling halls is to make profit, and these messages of responsibility are more than simple gestures of responsibility or public relations. Quitting the game altogether is not encouraged, as this would affect their income.

It is understandable that I had reservations about taking these leaflets seriously, as personal experience and losses suffered convinced me of the negative effects of gambling. However, I felt I could live with addiction.
I can't go on anymore and I have to take concrete steps to change my life. I picked up a flyer promoting help quitting gambling and found useful information that led me to the decision to pull myself out of an extensive database to quit the habit of gambling and find myself.
It was an essential step to improving life. I registered the phone number on the flyer, knowing that I needed help and guidance on this journey to quit gambling, a bold and vital step towards a better path and a more balanced life. A life free from gambling addiction.
Now I am determined to focus my energy and resources on building. I know it won't be easy, but I'm ready to face challenges and find ways to improve my quality of life by accepting help and giving my best. I can turn a fight into a success story if I commit to growth.

Every step I take now to quit gambling is a step towards a life full of happiness and fulfillment. It is essential to be critical and aware of the gambling industry's marketing messages and tactics in order not to fall into the trap of limited earnings and illusions of fun and seek professional help and support from appropriate sources such as gambling addiction groups. Take back control of your recovery process and your life.
Online virtual platforms have been the new dimension of my gambling addiction. We spent a lot of time and money on virtual online environments, which made it hard to do and limit. I laid my trap. I could control everything with the help of a gambling app on my phone. My reality was completely different. I was losing myself in this virtual world and everyone around me. My phone has become the gateway to constant betting and risk adventures. Everything became so easy with access to my account and games on the same device. A few taps on the phone screen were enough, and money disappeared through my fingers like instant sand. For me, the phone has become a gateway to loss and despair.
I have a lot of online accounts on most gambling platforms in the UK and Romania, and for the big screen I connect my laptop to the TV and sometimes let it play automatically. I have a strategy. It was the one where I would play with the dealer and slowly accumulate very few small winnings during the week and then more on weekends to have a controlled approach to gambling. If you want to enter a gambling site from another country, it is not possible, but with the creation of a VPN, it is possible, and you have to be very creative.
However, this approach devastated my bank account; Within hours, all the winnings I had accumulated during the week were gone, plus extra money. It's a harsh lesson learned that gambling can somehow take unexpected turns.
I have information and resources available from online gambling to help me in this process. I followed the steps, and requesting my withdrawal from the online platform was a testament to my commitment and determination to change my life by limiting my focus, resources and more valuable things.
It is essential to understand that online gambling can be just as dangerous and addictive as traditional gambling. Taking steps to protect ourselves from the online gambling environment is an

important step to regain control and live in a healthier environment.

The experience of losing large amounts of money in online gambling shows that addiction is not limited to a particular environment or type of gambling. It is essential to be aware of this and act accordingly. It is also necessary to find ways to spend your free time in a healthy and productive way. You may discover other interests, hobbies, or activities that give you personal satisfaction and fulfill your energy. You can overcome the disorder and create a more balanced and happy life with proper support.

After taking a break from gambling, life became a little boring. Then a small shop with betting machines appeared nearby. I thought, if I play the low stakes, that's fine. I started with small bets, but soon played more prominently and the limits hit me.

I kept playing until I had nothing left. Gambling seems easy, but most of the time it takes all your money. Surprisingly, I didn't even track how much I bet or how much I won.

But when you keep track of victories and defeats, it can be surprising. Remember, casinos and betting venues are designed to favor them in the long run, so it's essential to be aware. But when you monitor your profits and losses, you'll be surprised. So it is necessary to understand that gambling always has casinos or long bookmakers designed to favor and have periods. Players usually lose more than they win, although occasionally you can win. The total amount wagered and lost will be greater than the profit. Keep an eye out so you can analyze the results more objectively.

Also, check that when we get caught up in the temptation to gamble, we don't realize how much time and money we lost in the process, but when we stop and think, we realize it. Now we have nothing. We have lost many precious things, such as hope and our relationship with the love of our life, and now we cannot redeem them. I lost everything to games for 17 years.

I remember the days when I spent sleepless nights in front of the screen, neglecting personal and professional responsibilities, all because of the obsessive desire to earn more; With each losing bet, I told myself that the next one I could get lucky and recoup my losses, but this evil practice was a pitiful waste of money and time.

I admit that it was hard for me to accept that I had self-destructive habits and was wasting so much precious time. I felt further and further away, and I became detached.

When you realize how much time and money you've wasted gambling, there's a sense of foreboding and despair. You wonder what your life would have been like if you had channeled these precious resources in other directions. You may have had a successful career, or you may have traveled to exotic places and had much better relationships. Be strong and you will grow up in a perfect society.

It is important not to blame ourselves for our past mistakes and choices, but to look ahead and take responsibility for the change we can bring to our problems. Let's find ways to turn those things that give us complete fulfillment into absolute satisfaction.

With the right support, we can learn to regain control of our time and money and focus on personal growth, healthy relationships, and goals that bring us genuine happiness. But it's a worthwhile effort to get our lives back and make the most of the precious time we have.

I realize, as I reflect on these moments in my life, that fighting gambling addiction involves gradually removing the various obstacles that have held me captive to this evil, after I realized that money is a constant source of temptation. I decided not to carry cash with me anymore. However, effective action gave me an additional barrier against gambling. I no longer had money to attract me to a simple gaming hall or slot machines. It wasn't enough, I had to find practical ways to protect myself.

During a difficult and downright frustrating time, I was in this constant quest to break some not-so-great habits. As the clock kept ticking, I began to see that my usual tactics, trying to set boundaries and unleash things, were useless in the face of the strong pull of my desire to play. No matter how hard I tried, my luck didn't change, and quitting this bad habit proved to be challenging.

That's when I realized: I needed more than rules; I needed a change. I asked for help and went to therapy. Feeling better meant admitting it, making more brilliant moves around money, and focusing on positive things.

As I worked through all this, I began to see life differently. There is a lot of joy and satisfaction outside of the gambling world. Slowly but surely, I began to take the reins of my life back, imagining a future without being tied to addiction.

I learned that therapy wasn't just about solving the surface problems of addiction; It was about learning how to recompose my life without falling back into old habits. I saw that gambling was just my way of temporarily scratching off that creative itch and staying away from some difficult emotions.

I learned that gambling addiction can be the result of deep-rooted psycho-emotional and social factors, such as anxiety, depression, stress or relationship problems. The therapists guided me through a process of self-discovery and healing, where I explored why I played and the impact it had on my life.

Managing, finding changes in my life and meeting learning needs to experience happiness and fulfillment in other aspects of my life.

During therapy, I had the opportunity to understand concepts such as self-control, money management and setting realistic goals. I've learned support networking skills from people who do. Realizing and accepting that recovery from gambling addiction takes time and commitment to achieve it gave me the patience and perspective I needed to face challenges and continue to build a healthy and balanced life. It wasn't about getting rid of it, it was about regaining trust and making positive choices. It was about rediscovering one's identity.

Although my progress in therapy was a complex and complicated process, I had people who supported and encouraged me during difficult times. I can say that we have made significant progress against gambling addiction.

Despite slow progress, there were times when the urge to play reignited. It is important to note that the desire to gamble can be triggered by certain factors, such as stress at work and in personal life or tension and quarrels in relationships, and people often seek gambling as an escape from these situations. I was relieved that I could no longer enter the betting halls, but I was still tempted to go to the small bookmakers on street corners or near those places where I felt it was too risky. A possible source can fall into the trap of addiction at any time.

I have taken the necessary steps to distance myself from these small bookmakers. Although it was not a possible exit and I could not guarantee that I would not enter again, I understood that this was the right direction. We must be vigilant and determined in our fight for recovery.
My exit from the betting room was a solid commitment to building my own life without addiction. At the time, I was looking for healthy alternatives to meet my needs for recreation and relaxation.

I searched for hobbies and interests that would occupy my time and give me satisfaction and fulfillment. I found pleasure in reading, participated in sports activities and spent time in other constructive activities. I spent more time with friends and family and tried to reevaluate the trauma.
Even after I decided to quit gambling, I found that I still found ways to keep playing, either in betting halls or lesser-known places. Although I was aware of the restrictions imposed and knew that it was not in my best interest to continue, the temptation to try my luck was too great. Entering a casino, I started playing with only £20, but luck smiled on me and I soon accumulated £400. This victory made me feel satisfied and captivated by the excitement of winning, making me forget about the dangers of the game. That night, the feeling of euphoria and the desire to win more pushed me to keep playing, fueling my addiction even more.
At that moment, I was completely absorbed in the game screen, captivated by the excitement of victory, when suddenly someone shouted my name from behind. I turned quickly, meeting the gaze of a lady who asked me if I was the person I was looking for. In that moment of joy, I had completely forgotten my intention to leave and did not realize how deeply gambling controlled me. The woman brutally brought me back to reality, reminding me of my decision to self-exclude from the game. He strongly suggested that I collect my winnings and leave the place.
The meeting was brief, although it was a slap in the face, a moment of awakening in which I realized how captivated I was by this world of betting. At that moment, I realized that the restrictions imposed on me and my expulsion from the casino were not mere formalities, but measures designed to protect me

and help me free myself from the gambling addiction, for which I had broken the rules. The feeling of shame and disappointment with myself for returning to the game, knowing that I was already known in this situation and that surveillance measures were in place to prevent my access, made me feel vulnerable. Was my addiction previously known to be exposed and the hidden consequences?
The request to quit gaming was a wake-up call for me. There was a time when I became more aware that I needed to stop gambling and reevaluate my life in a healthy and balanced way. We need to find ways to create. This episode inspired me to continue fighting gambling addiction and not allow myself to fall into its trap. I realized that facing the consequences and taking responsibility for my actions were necessary steps in my recovery and regaining control of my life.
Well, the shame started to grow, and I realized I had to find a way to break this destructive cycle. It is important to be more aware and seek appropriate help and support. These are essential and can provide expert support and advice. This was when I realized I needed to engage in intensive care and face my addiction again in a safe environment and with the support of professionals. This whole battle has taught me that recovery is a long-term process. There is action, and returning to old behaviors can be done quickly; Establishing a healthy relationship and building a solid support network requires a significant change in thinking and lifestyle.

An era without gambling

The pandemic has affected my gambling routine; The closure of gambling halls and subsequent activities forced me to face the absence of these activities in my life, despite the lack of access to gambling halls and the new pressing need. I was relieved that I had found alternative ways to spend the time and money saved from gambling and turned my attention to more constructive and healthy activities.
All the time and energy I devoted to developing new hobbies at home was a great way to occupy my mind and free time, while spending money more profitably than I had spent on gambling. Not playing was an opportunity for me to do self-reflection and review my past gaming behavior when I felt the urge to play again.
I tried this eight-month period where I didn't play. It was a time of change and freedom for me, allowing me to use the money I would have spent on betting on things that give me pleasure and long-term fulfillment.
You know, there was a time when I thought I had everything under control. I said to myself, "Keep yourself busy, don't even think about it." But somehow, those old habits have a cunning way of creeping back onto you. It's as if one day you're minding your own business and the next day you're overwhelmed by total boredom, not just a "I have nothing to do" boredom, but a deep and heartbreaking emptiness.
And in that silence, that's when the whispers began: "Just a small bet, it doesn't hurt," they said. It was like a little devil on my shoulder, pushing me to the edge. It seemed so innocent at first glance, just a bit of fun, right? But deep down, I knew it was the beginning of something I vowed never to return to.
I was there, in an inner struggle with myself, trying to cheat on my own system that I had established as a salvation from myself. I was about to make the same mistake again. But the moment I tried to access a gambling site and succumb to temptation, something unexpected happened - the safety measures I imposed on myself came to my aid. The site blocked me, reminding me of my previous decision to stop: "It is no longer

possible, you will not repeat this mistake." This moment was a clear sign that I had to stand firm in my decision to quit gambling. I can't even tell you what relief hit me. It was like holding my breath and finally being able to breathe again. I was grateful for that wall I had crashed into. He stood there like a quiet, strong friend who knew better, even when I didn't.

That moment was a victory. It proved that maybe I'm stronger than I think I am. It was a sign, loud and clear, that I was going forward, not backward. Sure, I got too close to the edge for comfort, but I didn't fall. And that's something to be proud of, right? These small victories keep me going, fighting for a life where I am in control, not gambling.

That was a revelation for me. It made me laugh at my previous stupidity and realize where I ended up quitting gambling; This period of rest and self-reflection strengthened my resolve to stay on the road to recovery and focus on my personal career goals. I am capable.

It is essential to recognize that the road to recovery can be difficult and fraught with obstacles. However, my experiences during this period have shown me that it is possible to overcome gambling addiction and lead a more balanced and happy life.

What a rollercoaster it was! For eight solid months, I was on top of the world: no gambling, no late nights at the casino, nothing. I thought I had given up this vice for good. But the truth is that I was fooled - on my own, no less. I fooled myself into thinking that I was over, that the old me was gone. But the label "compulsive gambler" stuck to me like glue.

Taking a break from everything, I thought I would have a new perspective on life. I was convinced that I would never fall into the same old trap again. But, you know what they say about the best plans. I was naïve and unprepared for the wave that hit me when life returned to "normal."

The pandemic changed the rules of the game for me; The reclosure of casinos and subsequent restrictions forced me to face the void left by the absence of gambling in my life. When casinos reopened, I was irresistibly drawn back into the whirlwind of action, empty pockets and crushed spirit. I returned to personal hell, and the consequences were devastating, not only for me, but also for my loved ones. The most painful part was the realization of lost time, a time I will never be able to recover.

Now, here I am, trying to pick up the pieces. The past is gone, of course, but the future? That's mine to format.

For you, readers who may be going through this struggle or want to avoid this life, I am sending you a message of encouragement to take action to stop wasting your time and resources on gambling. Start and find the right support to help you overcome addiction. There are support groups and resources available.

Don't lose hope and remember that you are strong. With determination and support, you can regain control of your life and create a happier and more balanced future by dedicating yourself to what really matters. It doesn't matter where you are at this stage; You need to focus on the future and not let the past or certain groups of people influence or criticize you.

Try to make more promises to yourself each day and look for opportunities to do positive things. Dream every night how you can contribute to the good of those around you. Be an integral part of the community. If you're not a gambler yourself, but you know someone who has a problem, try talking to that person to help them get out of this vicious cycle.

When life finally started to return to normal after the pandemic, I found myself slipping back into old patterns. I found myself on autopilot, heading straight to the tables without thinking. Then, in a moment of enlightenment, like a scene from a movie, the idea of AA meetings, where people find solace in sharing their stories, inspired me to look for something similar for gamblers.

The first step towards meetings was not easy. I felt like I was on the edge of a precipice, doubtful of my ability to jump. But I did. At those meetings, listening to others talk about their experiences, I found an echo of my own struggle. It was a somber but incredibly comforting revelation.

I realized that this kind of healing was free in every sense of the word, offering a freedom I hadn't felt in a long time. It wasn't about money, but about an invaluable exchange of support and understanding. My recovery wasn't supposed to be a solitary road. By sharing our burdens, we could ease them.

On our first date, emotion overwhelmed me. The simple room, with a circle of chairs and coffee boiling in the background, was

a stark contrast to the casino world. As I listened, I felt the space become more intimate, almost destined for my presence.
When it was my turn to speak, I overcame the hesitation and shared my own story. The sympathetic reactions and tacit support of others were healing. I found a sense of belonging and a thread of hope in this room full of strangers.
After this meeting, I felt enormous relief. The road ahead was daunting, but I felt I had a real chance to fight. There is strength in our solidarity and in our shared words. When I went out that night, the casinos no longer seemed appealing to me. I was no longer just a player; I was a person in recovery and I was not alone.
As I attended meetings, my enthusiasm grew. But life brought new challenges, and my schedule became an obstacle. Missing meetings wasn't just a scheduling conflict; I felt like I was missing an essential step in my healing process.
Realizing that this newly found connection escaped me because of the service was difficult. This commitment to recovery, which had begun to fill the gaps in my soul, was now under threat. I understood the necessity of work, but I also knew how vital this part of my healing process was.
Finding a balance between work and recovery became my new challenge, reminding myself that the road to a better version of myself requires dedication and adaptability.

First, complementary therapy

The game changed for me when I finally decided to sit down at a therapist's table. It wasn't just about taking money out of your wallet; It was about exploring my past with someone with the skills to help me navigate it. I felt from the beginning that this therapist was on my side, not because of the salary, but because he really wanted to see me overcome this obstacle. His office was a calm place, a refuge in my stormy life. It became my safe harbor, where I could drop anchor and talk about anything: the bright spots of childhood that seemed so far away, and the shadows that followed me into adulthood.

At first, the sessions felt like a walk on a wire over a canyon of old memories, each holding a mixture of fear and nostalgia. However, the therapist had this way of making the wire appear wider and more stable with each visit. It created a space where I could unfold my history piece by piece without feeling overwhelmed. As the days turned into weeks, I began to draw connections between my yesterday and today. I began to see how the echoes of my childhood influenced the person I was now, the person who found solace in the ups and downs of gambling. It was like assembling a puzzle, seeing the full picture of why I was seeking a refuge where the stakes were high but the gains were much deeper than their monetary value. Understanding the complexity of my past wasn't an excuse for where I had gotten, it was a map that guided me out of it. And that made all the difference. Each session was a step toward healing, not just to break a habit, but to repair the parts of me that had been destroyed for so long.

All six therapy sessions were like a breath of fresh air in a room confined for too long. I began to see things differently, to feel things I hadn't allowed myself to think about for years. There was a sense of progress, as if we were finally moving forward. But as the meetings piled up, so did the bills, and part of me started questioning everything. "Haven't we spent enough? Shouldn't I feel better now?" I said to myself. I convinced myself that I was ready, that I had the necessary tools, and that I could handle it on my own, with a little help from time to time. After all, therapy had given me a new perspective, right? So I interrupted the sessions. For several days, I felt confident, even proud. I thought I had everything under control, that I could stay on the edge of the gambling world without falling into it. But this sensation was short-lived. Attraction, haste and escape called me back with a vengeance. The voice in my head whispered seductive lies, reminding me that felt-covered tables and blinking machines were where I felt safest, where the noise of life faded into the background.

It was a harsh awakening when I realized that the voice was as convincing as ever. The safety I felt in gambling was an illusion, a temporary shelter that came with its storm. It was a hard pill to swallow, seeing how quickly the feeling of control slipped through my fingers and how quickly the old gambling sanctuary tried to pull me back in.

I had to admit that the road to recovery wasn't as straight or short as I had hoped. The journey was longer, with more twists and turns than I would have prepared. But this stumble was not the end. It was just another part of the process. I had to remind myself that healing is not linear and that every step, even backward steps, taught me something vital. On a seemingly ordinary day, I received a phone call that would have a significant impact on my road to recovery. The voice on the other end of the line was that of a girl who introduced herself as a member of the organization where I had received my first treatment. There was something strange about her tone as the conversation continued. I found out she was Romanian. The constant question was, "What are you doing? How do you deal with gambling?" Deep down, I knew I was still in trouble. In this moment of continued honesty, I said I wanted to start therapy again.

With a familiar voice but an unexpected desire for awareness and openness to help, this phone call was my small step toward recovery. It was an important step. Time has passed since then, and regular therapy sessions have improved my life. Engaging in self-discovery and healing was a completely new experience for me. I felt connected and supported by my therapist. He belonged to Romania and spoke my mother tongue, which added a sense of familiarity and comfort during the sessions. I continued to explore memories and traumas from my past, which, although sometimes painful, helped me understand the deep roots of my gambling addiction. Therapy gave me an understanding environment where I could share my experiences and feelings without fear of being judged. During the sessions, we worked together to identify and explore the triggers that led me to resort to gambling, being able to choose and repress the addiction itself. In the course of therapy, I discovered other aspects of my life that needed attention and change. I explored my relationships, communication patterns and self-esteem, forming a new set of values and priorities to guide me.

Over time, I realized that recovery is not limited to therapy sessions, but also requires personal commitment, self-awareness, and regular self-care practices. I learned to take steps forward, face challenges, and find new ways to live a balanced and fulfilling life.

Therapy helped me redefine my value system and create a more balanced mindset. I gained confidence in myself and my ability to make healthy choices. One of the most valuable experiences was discovering myself more deeply and learning to appreciate the true richness of life: health, love, authentic relationships and the joy of living in the present moment.

In the end, it doesn't matter how many obstacles I encountered on my journey to recovery, it matters my strength and determination to celebrate my next birthday and create a better future for myself by realizing that the past is the past.

During abstinence sessions, I looked for ways to avoid playing again and protect myself from relapse into my gambling addiction. I decided to exclude myself from all online gambling platforms, starting with the UK and now in Romania. I contacted the operators and requested my removal from all gambling sites. This was essential to limit my ability to gamble and protect my finances. In addition, I have taken steps in the physical environment, such as eliminating banknotes and eliminating carrying bags on the go, to eliminate the possibility of spending money and finding creative solutions to manage my finances.

Over time, the list of these places expanded and I was subjected to almost 300 restrictions, which brought me closer to my goal of preventing access to gambling and eliminating temptation.

Overall, every step I took to limit my access to gambling was a step towards healing and an investment in a healthy and happy future.
I have reached a point in my life where I realize that gambling has brought me nothing but pain and despair. Now is the time to end this vicious circle and begin a new stage of awakening and healing in my life. My self-confidence grows and I have the power to create a more fulfilling future. I promise to use it. A ray of hope for quitting and health will prove appropriate, and my story will make a difference in people's lives.
It is essential to understand that time is precious and irrecoverable. Lost money and moments of frustration, whose words cannot be withdrawn, are real losses. However, we have learned that we can recover much lost ground through determination and action. This understanding comes from my practice and I aim to lay the foundations for a better, more fulfilled and balanced life.
By sharing these lessons with others, providing support and guidance, showing people that they are not alone in this battle and that there are many resources and communities available for help. This can play a key role in overcoming addiction.
The decision to seek therapy was a significant turning point in my journey. It marked the end of denial and the beginning of a path to healing. Entering the therapist's office for the first time, I had a mixture of apprehension and hope. This wasn't just a step towards addressing my gambling addiction; It was an adventure into the uncharted territories of my psyche. The therapist's office felt like a sanctuary, a stark contrast to the chaotic world I was used to. It was a space that promised understanding and support, a rare commodity in my tumultuous life.

Therapist: "Welcome. I understand that this may be a difficult step for you. How do you feel about being here today?"

Me: "Honestly, I'm nervous. I'm not used to talking to anyone about my gambling. It's always been my secret burden."

Therapist: "No, no, no: "It's normal to be nervous about openness. Do not forget that this is a safe space. Can you tell me what motivated you to seek help now?"

Me: "I think I've reached a point where I can't ignore this anymore. It affects everything, my work, my relationships and my life."

Therapist: "Recognizing the impact is a crucial first step. Let's talk about when you first noticed that gambling became more than just an occasional activity."

Me: "It's hard to say exactly when. It was gradual, you know? But now, it's like living a double life."

Therapist: "This feeling of living a double life can be stressful. Let's explore these two sides and understand what fulfills your gambling."

Me: "I've never thought of it that way before. I think it's an escape. When I gamble, I don't have to think about my problems."

Therapist: "Using gambling as an escape is quite common. Together, we can find healthier ways to meet life's challenges."

Me: "I'm not even sure where to start. My life is a disaster."

Therapist: "It's nothing. Recovery is a journey; We will go through it together, step by step. Today, we're starting by laying the groundwork."

This initial conversation with the therapist opened doors to a world I had kept closed for so long. A deep, sometimes painful, but ultimately transformative journey began. My journey through therapy was an odyssey into the depths of my psyche, a series of explorations that revealed insights essential to my recovery. These sessions, each a chapter of self-discovery, gradually pieced together the fragmented mosaic of my life.

One of the first sessions focused on the genesis of my gambling habit. The therapist's question, "What first attracted you to gambling?" transported me back to my first forays into gambling. It was not an inherited hobby or family tradition, but an adventure born of curiosity and the search for emotions. This session highlighted how gambling began innocently, a social effort that gradually turned into an escape mechanism from the stresses of life.

In the following sessions, I delved into the dual nature of gambling in my life. "How does gambling serve you?" the therapist asked me. As I reflected, I realized it was a double-edged sword—providing temporary relief from life's pressures while creating even more bottomless abysses of stress and guilt. It was an adaptation mechanism that went wrong, providing short-lived euphoria followed by prolonged despair.

One particularly emotional session revolved around the relationship between my self-esteem and gambling. "Do you feel validated by gambling?" was the question that touched on a sore point. I realized that gambling had become a yardstick for my self-esteem. Every win boosted my ego, and every loss was a crushing blow to my sense of self. This perception was a turning point that led me to seek validation beyond the realm of gaming tables and slot machines. I also explored the impact of my addiction on my relationships. "How has gambling affected your connections with others?" This question forced me to face the reality of strained relationships and missed opportunities. It was a cruel realization that my gambling was not a solitary activity, but had chain effects, affecting those I cared about.

One of the most challenging sessions was the one in which we approached the topic of change. "How do you feel about recovery?" the therapist asked me. This question made me reflect deeply on what I was really looking for from recovery. It wasn't just the cessation of gambling; It was a desire for a new sense of purpose, healthier coping mechanisms, and restored relationships.

Through these therapy sessions, I learned to identify and understand the triggers underlying my gambling habit. I dissected moments of stress, loneliness, and insecurity, linking them to my impulses to play. The therapist taught me strategies to counteract these triggers, such as seeking social support, engaging in hobbies, and practicing mindfulness.

Each therapy session was an important step in demystifying my addiction. I began to discover the complicated web of psychological, emotional, and social factors that fueled my gambling. This understanding was crucial because it changed my perspective, moving from self-blame to self-knowledge, thus paving the way for genuine healing and transformation.

During these sessions, I found the courage to face my vulnerabilities and the strength to forge a new path. The insights

I gained were not just revelations about my addiction, they were beacons that guided me to a new horizon.

The insights from the therapy sessions gradually permeated every aspect of my daily life. Each revelation in therapy translated into tangible changes, reshaping my habits, decisions, and lifestyle in general.

One of the most significant changes has been in the way we manage stress. Before therapy, stress was a direct ticket to gambling as a means of escape. However, through treatment, I learned healthier coping mechanisms. I started practicing mindfulness and meditation. These practices have helped me stay grounded and present, reducing the overwhelming need to find solace in gambling.

My approach to social interactions and relationships has also transformed. I learned to be more open and honest in my communication, especially with close friends and family. Where I once isolated myself, I now sought the support and company of my loved ones. This helped me feel more connected and supported when I was tempted to gamble.

Financial management has been another area that has seen a drastic change. Therapy helped me understand the value of financial responsibility and the dangers of impulsive spending, a common trait on my gaming days. I started budgeting and tracking my spending, which kept my finances in check and gave me a sense of control and accomplishment.

One of the most subtle but profound changes has been in my daily routine. I restructured my day to include activities that would fulfill me and align with my recovery goals. These included reading, engaging in neglected hobbies, and spending time in nature. These activities filled the void that gambling once occupied and brought a sense of joy and satisfaction into my life.

Therapy also instilled in me the importance of self-reflection. I kept a journal to document my thoughts, feelings, and experiences. This practice has become an invaluable tool for self-knowledge and tracking my progress. It helped me recognize patterns in my behavior and thoughts, making it easier for me to proactively address them.

In addition, therapy taught me to celebrate small victories. Every day without gambling, every successful trigger management was

a victory. Recognizing these milestones lifted my spirits and strengthened my commitment to recovery.
Change wasn't always easy, and there were days when old habits and temptations lurked nearby. However, the skills and insights in therapy have equipped me with the tools to navigate these challenges more effectively.
Essentially, the impact of therapy extended beyond simply addressing my gambling addiction. It prompted a holistic transformation, influencing the way I looked at and interacted with the world around me. It was a kind of reprogramming – from a life dictated by gambling to one driven by conscious and healthy choices.
Through these changes, I was not only working to overcome my addiction, but also to build a foundation for a more balanced and fulfilling life.
As my therapeutic journey progressed, one of the most transformative achievements I encountered was the importance of self-care and its profound impact on mental health. This realization was not an overnight revelation, but a gradual awakening to the needs and well-being of my mind and body.

As I learned in therapy, self-care extended far beyond the usual notions of relaxation and pampering. It was about nurturing myself, respecting my boundaries, and creating an environment conducive to healing and growth. This journey of self-care began with understanding and addressing my basic needs.
Sleep, which I had often neglected, became a cornerstone of my self-care routine. I set myself a regular sleep schedule, understanding that a rested mind was crucial to my decision-making and emotional stability. Food followed suit. I began to pay attention to what I ate, focusing on a balanced diet that would fuel my body and mind. This lifestyle change not only improved my physical health, but also had a positive impact on my mood and energy levels.
Exercise has become a regular part of my routine. Activities such as jogging, going to the gym, and even simple walks in the park have become vital for their therapeutic effects. Exercise was no longer just a matter of fitness, but became a means of releasing

tension, clearing the mind, and achieving a sense of accomplishment.

Mental health has been another critical aspect of my self-care journey. I started practicing mindfulness and meditation, which helped me stay anchored and present. These practices allowed me to observe my thoughts and feelings without judging them, giving me a clearer perspective on my internal states. They became essential tools in impulse management and in reducing the anxiety and stress that often led to gambling.

As part of my self-care routine, journaling was a reflective practice. It was a safe space where I could express myself freely, process my emotions, and track my progress. Writing in my journal became a daily ritual that gave me insight and clarity into my mental and emotional states.

Another aspect of self-care was learning to set boundaries with others and myself. This meant saying no to environments or situations that triggered my impulses to play and being aware of my limits. Setting these boundaries was challenging, but it was essential to maintain my recovery and mental well-being.

Engaging in hobbies and activities that brought me joy and fulfillment was also a form of self-care. Rediscovering and exploring old interests added richness and diversity to my life. These activities gave me a sense of purpose and a counterbalance to the emptiness left by gambling.

Importantly, self-care also involves seeking professional help when needed. Recognizing that therapy is an ongoing process, I maintained regular sessions and checkups with my therapist. This ongoing support has been crucial to navigating the complexities of recovery and maintaining my mental health.

The culmination of these self-care practices led to a profound improvement in my overall well-being. It wasn't just about recovering from gambling addiction; It was about rebuilding and fortifying myself. I learned to listen to my body and mind, treat myself with kindness and compassion, and take proactive steps to maintain my mental health.

This self-care journey was proof that recovery is multifaceted. It's not just about ending an addiction, it's about nurturing your whole being. I became more balanced, resilient, and self-aware as I adopted these practices.

The lessons I learned in therapy and my self-care practices created a synergy that propelled me toward a healthier, more fulfilling life. I realized that self-care was not a luxury, but a necessity, a fundamental aspect to living a life free from the chains of addiction.

As I reflect on this journey, I am reminded of the deep strength and resilience within each of us. My story, marked by challenges and triumphs, is a testimony to the power of self-care in transforming lives. It is a journey that continues, each day being a step towards a healthier and more mindful existence.

By sharing these reflections, I hope to inspire others on their journey to recovery. To show that with dedication, support and a commitment to self-care, it is possible to overcome addiction and lead a healthy, happy and fulfilling life.

Anonymous group therapy

If you find yourself in a similar situation, I encourage you to get the help you need. Do not hesitate to talk to professional therapists. Make sure that every step towards recovery counts and that you deserve to live a happy life.

A "Gamblers Anonymous" (support group for players in recovery) in the UK was a life-changing for me. I decided to attend the morning meeting. I was received in the meeting with an open heart. People shared their experiences and we found that the group was supportive. They were there for me and others, giving us a sense of community and understanding. I was not alone in my struggle; Each of us had a work story and had to live to the limits of gambling. I realized that there is no judgment, only unconditional support and understanding.

During the sessions, we learned the stories of suffering, struggle and success of other members. I realized that there is a path to recovery and that we can walk it together. Having already been part of this journey, I realized that there is hope for a better life. At Gamblers Anonymous I found a strong support network where I could share my fears and successes. Band learned that I wasn't alone in what I was going through and that there were resources and tools to help me stay on the road to recovery.

The lack of gambling can undoubtedly be debated about the emotion and power of the message and can become an inspiration for all libertarians. And it provides understanding.

As time passed, I began to feel different. I noticed that most of the participants were already recovering. My English was not the best. Being among them, being the only one who didn't speak English as a first language, made me feel very different, and not in a good way. I was afraid of being criticized and ostracized. I used to feel that way. It made me feel isolated and insecure about my place in the group. I was able to rebuild, but at the same time, I knew I was struggling with this addiction myself.

English, spoken with an authentic British accent, contributed to my sense of belonging and alienation. His enthusiastic and frank discussion of progress reminded me of the long and challenging road ahead. I will be able to completely free myself from this evil.

Despite this anxiety and reluctance, I had the opportunity to share my personal story. I had a chance to share my story. Initially, I hesitated, but I opened up about my struggles. I appreciated others' decisions not to speak up, which gave me the confidence to make my story safer over time.
In the end, the meeting I attended was an unforgettable experience. Although mysterious, I felt part of a powerful group, aware of personal differences and challenges. I had to overcome my struggles with addiction. However, I appreciate being able to choose when and how to share the story.
Despite feelings of bitterness and despair, I decided to leave the support group. Try to recognize and learn from it.
I was as honest as ever about my absence from meetings and admitted that although I didn't have a gambling group, I still suffered from temptation. It was a sign of weakness and I hoped the group would take care of it. And he will continue to support me.
Despite the fact that there are no quick fixes, I continue to participate, realizing that each step brings me closer to freedom. My goal is self-growth, learning from mistakes and dedicating myself to healing.
I know it can't be easy and challenges lie ahead, but I think I will find the right support and a path to separation together. I will live without gambling.
The feeling of being lied to repeatedly made me believe and feel deaf that as long as I continued to face the truth and take responsibility for my actions, I could leave my recovery without progress. There was an obstacle in my way and I had to overcome it. For my treatment to be successful, I had to be honest with myself and the group. I learned to have an open mind and find the support that fits my needs. It is essential to see where I find support on my recovery journey.
Even better, I'm still trying to find the best way to stop gambling, and I know it's hard. I have to use different methods to solve the problem. I am determined to keep going until I have enough support to overcome my addiction. It's not easy, but I have to stick to it.

At first, I didn't think getting help worked, but I realized it was necessary. It was hard for me, but I turned to GamCare. They asked me questions to understand how serious my problem was. I haven't thought about suicide, but I know some people do it when they lose everything because of gambling.

Even though at first I wasn't sure about GamCare (an independent UK charity that provides advice and support to everyone affected by gambling damage), I found it helpful. I needed early help to overcome my gambling problem. I'm glad I didn't let thoughts of revenge or suicide take over my life.
I started reading books and talking to a therapist. It was hard, but it helped me understand why I was playing and how to stop. The recovery process is challenging, but I can build a better life with the right attitude.
I've heard stories of people losing everything because of gambling. That made me realize I couldn't take it lightly. I have to admit that I have a problem and ask for help. Asking for help is not a weakness; It is necessary. I couldn't beat addiction on my own, so I got help from professionals.
The therapists helped me find out why I was playing. The road to recovery has been hard, but I have seen improvements. I realized that I was weak and needed others to stay on the right path. Gambling addiction is a common problem and there are resources and communities to help.
Phone therapy was good, but I needed more. I found local support groups and meetings of Gamblers Anonymous. Sharing my story and listening to others' stories helped me. I needed solid support to rebuild my life and avoid returning to gambling.
I continued to learn about my addiction in support groups. I faced challenges, doubted myself, and sometimes relapsed, but kept moving forward. Today, I am on the road to recovery, building a new life without gambling. I hope my story inspires others to find a way to live a healthy life. I am back in therapy with GamCare via video conferencing for more support and connection.
At the heart of my struggle with gambling addiction, the group Gamblers Anonymous has become more than just a therapy session; It turned into a haven of shared experiences and tacit understanding. Each meeting was a tapestry of stories woven from the threads of our collective struggles, hopes and resilience.

I remember very well the first time I shared my story. My voice trembled, words stumbled with fear of judgment. But when I looked around the room, I saw signs of understanding, eyes that reflected my fears and struggles.
It was Michael, a middle-aged man whose journey mirrored mine. His stories about struggling with the urge to gamble, about nights spent in front of slot machines, resonated deeply with me. He talked about his family, about the pain he saw in his wife's eyes, which echoed the guilt I harbored in my heart. In his words, I found a mirror of my soul. His struggles, his small victories, became a source of strength for me. He taught me that recovery is not a solitary struggle, but a shared journey.
Then there was Emma, a young woman whose bright smile hid the depth of her addiction. Her courage to face her demons inspired me. He talked about gambling as an escape, a feeling I knew all too well. But her determination to change, to regain her life, struck a chord in my soul. Emma's journey was a testament to the power of hope and strength of the human spirit.

These connections formed the foundation of my recovery. In their stories, I found pieces of my story and saw the possibility of change in their travels. The group became a microcosm of support and understanding, a place where the weight of judgment was lifted and the burden of addiction was shared.

A bond formed over weeks and months as we shared our ups and downs, victories and failures. A bond forged in the heat of shared adversity. In this modest room, surrounded by people who were once strangers, I found a sense of community. A community that understood the language of addiction, the silent cries for help, and whispers of hope that were often not heard.

Group therapy wasn't just about sharing our stories; It was about building a support system, a network of people who had traveled the same treacherous path and emerged stronger. It was about learning from each other, drawing strength from our collective experiences, and finding solace in not being alone in our struggles.

As I listened and shared in each session, I felt the walls I had built around me slowly crumble. I learned to trust, open up, and accept help. It was in this space of vulnerability and openness that I began to heal. The stories of connection and support I found in the group Gamblers Anonymous weren't just narratives; They were lifelines, pulling me back from the brink of despair and guiding me to a path of recovery and hope.

As I continued to attend Gamblers Anonymous meetings, a subtle but profound transformation began to unfold within me. It was a journey of self-discovery that led me down winding paths of introspection and self-awareness. In the early days of my therapy, I saw myself as just a victim of my circumstances, trapped in an addiction I thought I couldn't control. My self-perception was clouded by feelings of guilt, shame, and a deep-rooted sense of failure.

However, as I listened to the others in the group, I gradually began to see myself in a different light. Each session was like holding a mirror in front of my inner self, reflecting on my weaknesses and potential for change. I remember a special session where one member, an elderly gentleman named John, talked about how he had learned to redefine his identity beyond addiction. His words struck a chord in my mind. He talked about recognizing and accepting different facets of his personality that were overshadowed by gambling.

Inspired by John's ideas, I began to explore the parts of myself that I had neglected. I realized I was more than just my addiction; I was a person with dreams, talents and the capacity for joy and love. This realization was both liberating and daunting. It meant taking responsibility not only for my recovery, but also for rediscovering and nurturing my true self.

In this newly discovered journey of self-perception, I began to confront my past decisions and actions. I recognized the harm I had caused myself and my loved ones, and this recognition was painful but necessary. It was a process of peeling back layers of denial and rationalization to confront the harsh truth of my situation.

Gradually, I began to appreciate small victories, daily moments of strength and endurance. I celebrated the days I resisted the urge to play, the times I chose to reach out to a friend instead of succumbing to isolation. These moments have become milestones in my journey, each of which is a testimony to the evolution of my self-perception.

As I became more aware of my strengths and weaknesses, I became more compassionate towards myself. I understood that recovery was not a linear path, but a journey with ups and downs. This realization brought with it a sense of peace. I became more patient and forgiving of myself, recognizing that each day was an opportunity for growth and healing.

The evolution of my self-perception was not only about overcoming gambling, but also about redefining my identity. It was about building a new self based on self-respect, resilience and hope. This journey has not been an easy one. It required constant effort and introspection, but it was a journey that ultimately led me to greater self-understanding and acceptance.

In the group Gamblers Anonymous, I found a space where I could let go and rebuild my sense of self. It was a place where I could get rid of the labels of "gambler" or "addict" and be myself in all my complexity and potential. This evolution of self-perception was a crucial step in my recovery, a step towards living not only without gambling, but also towards living with purpose and authenticity.

Overcoming challenges: The power of courage in lives

As far as I understand, history is replete with stories of individuals whose extraordinary achievements were not solely due to their intelligence. More often than not, their courage set them apart, making a real difference in the world. This perspective is significant for those facing challenges such as gambling addiction. Overcoming these obstacles doesn't just mean understanding the problem intellectually; It's about having the courage to face them and defeat them.

Courage means facing fear, pain, danger, and uncertainty. It's about choosing to act despite the risks, embracing the unknown, and valuing effort, regardless of the outcome. Intelligence is undeniably essential, but without courage, it remains dormant. Courage brings brilliance to life, stimulating it into meaningful actions.

Think of historical figures like Martin Luther King Jr. and Nelson Mandela. Intelligence guided them, but the courage with which they faced daunting odds truly defined them. They stood up against injustice with an unwavering spirit that inspires us.

In science and innovation, personalities such as Marie Curie and Thomas Edison combined their intellectual abilities with the courage to venture into uncharted territory. Their remarkable discoveries were the result of both their audacity and their intellect.

When it comes to overcoming addictions such as gambling, this principle becomes even more vital. Intelligence alone is often not enough; The courage to acknowledge the problem, seek help, face social stigma and embark on the arduous road of recovery really matters.

The stories of those who fought and overcame their addictions often emphasize the importance of courage. It is visible in their first steps toward seeking help, resisting temptation, and traveling toward rebuilding their lives.

Courage manifests itself in various aspects of life, such as starting a new career, moving to a new country, or leaving a toxic relationship. For someone struggling with gambling addiction, it could be as simple as saying no to a trip to the casino or investing time in a healthier hobby. These acts, however small, accumulate to produce profound changes.

For those who are on the path to recovery or personal growth, remember: your courage is just as crucial, if not more, than your intelligence. It's the catalyst that drives you to take steps toward your goals. While brilliance can light the way, courage is what keeps you moving forward on it.

Intelligence, while a valuable trait, is often eclipsed by courage when it comes to achieving genuine success. In the face of life's difficulties, it is essential to remember that our true ally is courage. It gives us the strength to overcome addictions, radically change our lives and achieve excellence. The examples left by prominent personalities show us that, although intelligence is of significant importance, courage is often the key to expressing one's potential to the fullest.

His story was a stark reminder of the dangers of gambling – not just financial ruin, but also the emotional and psychological toll it takes. It highlighted the impact on families, lost moments with children and broken promises to loved ones. This man's life, consumed by the relentless pursuit of gain, was a touching example of the cost of addiction.

Even in the darkest chapters of our lives, there is always a glimmer of hope, a possibility for change. This became evident in the continuing story of the man I met in the UK, the hardworking individual consumed by the gambling world. Despite the initial sense of despair surrounding his story, a subtle shift loomed on the horizon.

In our numerous meetings, I had suggested that he seek help, mentioning anonymous groups for gamblers and the possibility of excluding himself from gambling places and sites. At the time, my words seemed to disappear into the void of his despair, with no apparent impact. However, once sown, the seeds of change can sometimes take root in the most barren lands.

I continued to work with him, attracted by his tireless work ethic and impressions of the person who could be beyond gambling. About a year later, during one of our routine conversations, he shared with me news that was music to my ears. He had taken his first steps to break free from the chains of gambling. He had begun to exclude himself from gaming venues and online platforms, a significant step toward regaining control of his life.
But the changes didn't stop there. He began to harbor new ambitions. He had learned to drive and was saving money for a car. This was more than a practical objective; symbolized his new direction and his purpose rediscovered. His words resonated deeply and filled me with a cautious sense of hope. He gave credit to our conversations, to my words, for helping him see the possibility of a different life, a life in which gambling was no longer the central axis.
His journey reflected the pattern I had seen repeatedly, including in my own life. The road to recovery from gambling addiction is often long and winding, requiring patience, time and external support. It's a path where progress can be slow and sometimes invisible, but every small step counts.

His story was evolving, not just a story of loss and despair, but also of resilience and change. It was a reminder that the grip of gambling can be loosened and that lives can be redirected to healthier, more satisfying paths. His progress was a testimony to the power of support, to the fact that someone believes in you even when you have lost confidence in yourself.
As he talked about his plans for the future, I couldn't help but feel a sense of pride and hope. His story was becoming one of recovery and renewal, a story that many players long to write for themselves. It strengthened my conviction that, with support and determination, change is always within reach, and a life free from the influence of gambling is not just a dream, but a possible reality.

Synthesis

On the gambling journey, a gambler like me becomes entwined in the exciting but treacherous terrain of gambling addiction. My story is not just an account of experiences; It is a profound exploration of the human spirit navigating the tumultuous waters of highs and lows, victories and failures, and the metamorphoses that define the struggle for recovery. My journey into gambling addiction reveals specific facets of this immersive and transformative experience.

At first, I introduced the reader to the seductive world of gambling. Initial encounters with the bookmakers' seductive charm set the stage for what evolved into an introspective realization of the addictive nature inherent in this quest.

As addiction worsened, it took desperate measures to break ties with the bookmakers' insidious allure. The challenges of guaranteeing a complete exit from the game have come to light, prompting an exciting exploration of recreational alternatives and the establishment of a vital support network.

Gambling took over my life, which made quitting difficult. Casinos were a big problem, tempting me to go back. An alarm signal made me aware of the consequences and take responsibility.

The pandemic turned my gambling routine upside down. The lockdown helped a bit, but it was hard to get back to gambling afterwards. Eight months without gambling taught me a lot. The fact that I thought I had "cured" led to a relapse. Intensive care and support were crucial to a sustainable recovery.

I joined Gamblers Anonymous for help. Group therapy has become essential for healing, even with challenges. Early help from GamCare added another level to my recovery.

Sharing stories in support groups was powerful. Gamblers Anonymous has provided me with strong support, helping me through my difficult journey to recovery.

Recovery is underway, with continuous learning and new priorities. Harnessing the newfound force for a better future offers hope.

Time is precious in recovery, and helping others struggling with addiction is essential. The final chapter looks back at the pain of gambling, emphasizing that quitting is a process, not a one-time decision. The hope is that sharing my story will guide others through similar struggles.

My story is just one of many. It is a testimony to my journey and a light of hope for those facing similar problems.

Part 2: Ways to quit gambling

"There is no victory without a fight. The greatest battle we have is with ourselves." – Napoleon Hill

Every morning, you wake up and feel regret, disappointment, and frustration. In every attempt to free yourself from gambling, sometimes you win, sometimes you lose; It seems to be a cycle that has no end. I assure you that you are not alone in these moments of struggle. Hope is the only thing navigating you to reach your destination.

This book is not only a guide on how to get rid of gambling addiction, it is more than that. It is like a light in the dark, a companion who never leaves you alone on the journey, an ally in battle. The book helps you transform, discover yourself and recover; It leads you to a happier and more successful life.

"It doesn't matter if you get knocked down, it matters if you get up." – Vince Lombardi.

Freedom from gambling addiction is not like reaching your destination, it's like a journey. There is no shortcut and no magic pill. But there is strong faith and hope. There is a power that can change your life. There is a happy life beyond gambling; That life awaits you.

Each step you take on this journey will bring you closer to the person you want to become or the ideal person you have in mind. You will face various obstacles; One day, you may be hopeless and wonder if change is possible. But in every moment, you will be with you.

Gambling may seem essential to your life right now, but it's not true. Life could be like a game. Sometimes you win, and sometimes you lose. You will enjoy it if you think from this perspective. It might give you a place where you feel safe, not where you continually live under the shadow of fear of further loss.

"The road to success is always under construction."

- Arnold Palmer

Of course, you will always find that the road to quitting gambling is under construction. This path is scary, but you will find joy, achievement, and moments of self-discovery.

The most important thing is that the destination of this path is a free life. So if you are eager to start this journey and want to take complete control of your life, you need to take responsibility and make the necessary changes in your life to quit gambling.

Then I invite you to turn the page. Let's start the journey together. Let us move much further down the road to a better, happier, healthier life and a path to freedom.

"When things go wrong, don't let yourself be defeated; beat things." – John Addison

Once you begin this journey, you will notice that you are not alone. However, you will be accompanied by support communities, therapy groups, family, friends and specialist counsellors who will help you begin the recovery process.

But it is all up to you, for you are the most essential part of this journey. It depends on your willingness to change, your mental and physical strength, determination, and reaction to obstacles that come your way. These are the powerful weapons you need to fight this battle. During the trip, if you feel tired, then do not forget why you started it in the first place. You want to recover, to live a life without gambling.

"The best investment you can make is in yourself." – Warren Buffett

The path to quitting gambling addiction leads you to self-discovery. You will face your inner fears, and your negative and positive thoughts will fight each other. You will win if you stay strong and don't let negative thoughts control you. After this victory, you will be a new and better version of yourself and you will not believe how strongly you ever thought possible.

Through this book, I will share my experiences, methods, and tips that helped me get out of this situation. I have mentioned in detail all my practical tips, techniques and strategies that help me quit gambling. No matter how complex your problem is, there is always a way out. And I will tell you exactly this way.

"Everything you want is on the other side of fear." - Jack Canfield

Ultimately, I hope this book will motivate you, give you hope for success, and encourage you to take the first step toward a new life. The life in which you will control your lives, not gambling. You can shape your destiny. A dream life where you can experience joy, fulfillment and peace.

Let us begin the journey; You will find me nearby. My tips and techniques will guide you every step of the way. I pray and wish to see you triumph, quit gambling and live a new life with joy and complete happiness.

"Any change, even a change for the better, is always accompanied by inconvenience." – Arnold Bennett.

Feelings of anxiety and fear are normal and part of this process. These feelings of fear are not evidence of failure, but proof that you are on the right track. Every fear is like an obstacle that you have to overcome; Once you cross each barrier, you will feel stronger and more able to quit gambling.

"It's never too late to be what you could have been." - George Eliot

So we must move forward to leave the past behind. We can't fix past failures, but we can make our future brighter and avoid the same kind of failure.

"Change is not a wheel that spins without moving, but a way forward. Forward, in a new, good direction." – Scott H. Young

In the following lines, we will explore a number of essential approaches and strategies for managing gambling addiction, including therapy, medication, support groups, and more. Each of these methods provides valuable tools to address this challenge from multiple perspectives. We will detail how each approach, from the support of medical professionals to the community one, can contribute to an efficient and sustainable recovery process.

Stress management: Therapy: Experts like therapists can help you cope. They can identify specific causes of gambling addiction and offer solutions to manage the urge to gamble. Detailed behavioral therapy is considered the best approach for the treatment of gambling addiction.

Support groups: Community support, such as support groups, can provide a support network. Within a group, people meet, share similar experiences, and offer suggestions for improvement. There are many such groups, an example being "Gamblers Anonymous" in the UK.

Medications: In some cases, medications prove to be the best way to manage addictions, such as gambling addiction. It is important to learn how you can use all these methods at once to fight addiction.

Blocking access to gambling: Various applications or programs can block access to gambling sites. This method may also be effective for some people.

Stress management techniques: Stress is dangerous and we should focus on various management techniques. The most well-proven methods of stress management include exercise and medication.

Financial planning: Poor financial conditions could trigger stress. So we need to do some financial planning to manage gambling debts, because these debts are one of the main reasons for continuing gambling. The financial advisor can help with this; However, tips and strategies also mention managing the ultimate debt pressure triggered by gambling.

Replacing gambling with positive activities: You can redirect your energy to some more productive ways instead of gambling. Describe those activities that can bring you joy and satisfaction.

Support from family and friends: Family and loved ones can play a crucial role in recovery. They provide emotional support and motivate individuals. Even some family members challenge you to do this.

"You cannot cross the sea just by standing and looking at the water." – Rabindranath Tagore.

All the methods mentioned above will be discussed in detail in this book. We will approach the topic in a comprehensive way, covering almost all personality types because each person is unique and what works for some may not work for others. Therefore, it is important to try all methods and choose the one that suits you best. Any change takes time, so it is suggested not to expect immediate results to avoid disappointments. It takes continuous efforts, courage and dedication to achieve your goals.

"The road to success and the road to failure are almost the same." – Colin R. Davis

As mentioned earlier, I will start with a detailed discussion of all methods. Please remember that every step, every effort and every route counts. If you're still reading the book and want to make a change, I'm here to support you in your aspiration for a gambling-free life.

Therapy

Therapy is the main step in the process of quitting gambling, giving us the causes and solutions to this problem. Professional experts can study your case. After thorough investigation, they can determine the main reasons for this addiction and how you can overcome these problems. The therapist will share strategies with you by using your inner and outer resources to deal with this problem and free us from this destructive addiction or, we can say, addiction.

An expert in the field may better suggest the solution instead of receiving an opinion from an ordinary person. So a therapist who specializes in gambling addiction treatment can really provide us with a safe and authentic setting. Through dialogue and exploration, we understand the dynamics of our addiction, triggers and dangers/threats related to these behaviors. Investigation is a crucial part of our recovery process. Discuss CBT, why it's essential, and how it helps us. CBT, "Cognitive-behavioral therapy," is the most effective therapy for treating gambling addiction.

CBT focuses primarily on identifying negative thoughts and turning them into positive comments. How does it work? Usually, through CBT, we learn to recognize and identify thoughts

negative/self-destructive and replace them with healthy alternatives, thus managing the need to play. This therapy not only helps us in the recovery process, but also solves underlying emotional issues that may contribute to gambling addiction. It helps us manage our negative thoughts, learn how to cope with stress, and helps us develop emotional regulation skills. With therapy, our vision expands, and we can find alternative ways to meet emotional needs and find satisfaction, joy, and inner peace in other aspects of our lives. A critical aspect of therapy is its personalized nature, tailored to each person's needs and experiences. The duration of therapy varies depending on the complexity of the individual situation and the progress made by the person. The therapist can be considered a reliable partner, providing support throughout the recovery journey. He guides us every step of the way, providing emotional support and positive feedback.

So choose the best therapist with an excellent track record in managing these issues. If you find the best therapist, consider that half of the problem is already solved, because you will be treated by them throughout the recovery process, taking into account your specific needs.

Support groups

In addition to individualized therapy, support groups are a valuable and essential resource for those struggling with gambling addiction. Participating in these groups provides a safe space to share thoughts and receive practical suggestions from other members. The benefits of being part of such groups are manifold. Group members connect, share their problems and challenges, creating a sense of solidarity and mutual support. Similar experiences of members can provide a sense of togetherness, reinforcing the belief that you are not alone in this struggle and that there are people who understand and support you. Successes and practical strategies shared in the group can serve as a source of inspiration and motivation, sparking a positive thought such as "If they can succeed, then so can I", which can motivate you to continue on your path to recovery. Another advantage of joining the group is that we can easily share our ideas and discuss our problems without fear of being judged because, in these groups, everyone is a victim and wants a solution to solve their problem. So everyone listens carefully to each other's stories and tries to figure out how they can overcome addiction. Sharing experiences can give us new perspectives and practical solutions to cope with temptations and build a gambling-free life.

The next important task is to find support groups. How can one discover support groups? These groups can be found through online searches, contacting social services, or through recommendations from mental health professionals. Even some freelance professionals in the mentioned field are also available on various online platforms. You just have to find the best one for you. So always look for support groups that have experience with gambling addiction and provide a safe and confidential environment for all group members. Helping others is not only good for others, it also strengthens our recovery. Participating in support groups can play an essential role in the healing process and give us all the support and inspiration we need on the path to a gambling-free life.

Medically

Medications are a valuable tool in the treatment of gambling addiction in certain situations. Although there is no magic pill for curing addiction, medication can be used as part of your treatment plan, along with therapy and other therapeutic approaches.

There are different types of drugs, adapted to individual needs, but their assessment is carried out by specialists. These include antidepressants, such as Fluoxetine or Sertraline, which can help manage stress, depression or anxiety associated with gambling by stabilizing mood and relieving emotional symptoms that occur during quitting gambling.

Other medications include opioid receptor antagonists, such as naltrexone, which can block receptors involved in the brain's reward system and reduce the level of pleasure associated with gambling. By blocking brain receptors, the need to play is also reduced.

A third type of medication is anticonvulsants, such as Topiramate, effective in reducing impulsivity and the desire to gamble by regulating brain activity. These medications can help control symptoms associated with gambling addiction.

It is important to understand that medications should not be considered a one-off solution to gambling addiction; instead, they should be used in combination with cognitive-behavioral therapy (CBT) and other forms of therapy to address the emotional and behavioral aspects of addiction.

It is imperative that you discuss your treatment plan with a doctor who specializes in this area so that he or she can develop a plan tailored to each person's needs and circumstances. After a thorough investigation and diagnosis, your doctor will recommend appropriate medications and adjust doses during regular follow-up checkups.

Always consider yourself the author of your own life story; It is essential to design your own path.

Stress management techniques

These techniques play a vital role in the recovery process. With these techniques, we can calibrate our emotions, relax, and manage the tension/stress associated with addiction efficiently and effectively.

Some fundamental stress management techniques are outlined below.

Deep breathing can calm and relax your mind during stressful times. The best practice is to breathe in slowly through your nose, hold your breath for 20-30 seconds, and exhale through your mouth. Repeat this activity 8 to 10 times. This will relax your mind and deliver oxygen to your entire body through your lungs.

Progressive muscle relaxation techniques: The action of contracting and relaxing different muscle groups in the body is called PMRT or "Progressive muscle relaxation techniques". You can start at the lower body with your toes and work your way up to your upper body, relaxing each muscle group. This technique is best for muscle relaxation.

Meditation and mindfulness: If you want to improve concentration and quiet your mind, meditation and mindfulness practices are excellent ways to achieve these goals. In everyday life, various meditation techniques, such as mindfulness and breath-focused meditation, prove to be among the most effective.

Regular exercise: It is scientifically proven that physical activity can have a positive impact on our emotional state thanks to a hormone called endorphin produced by our body during intense exercise. Gym, jogging, and sports are the various recommended physical activities you can try. You need to allocate at least 20-30 minutes daily.

Engage in hobbies and hobbies: Make a list of those activities that bring you joy, make these activities a regular part of your daily routine, and engage in them. There are various such activities, for example, painting, dancing, sports, hiking, cooking, reading, traveling and gardening; You can adopt any hobby that suits you and arouses your interest.

Time management and prioritization: Given that time is limited, we often face the need to perform multiple tasks, and sometimes we fail to fulfill all of them, including some of the most important responsibilities. To address this issue, it's effective to organize your time: create a list of daily activities and prioritize them according to urgency. Do the most urgent actions first and eliminate unnecessary activities. Prioritizing activities helps avoid overload and excessive pressure.

Socializing and connecting with other people: Emotional support and social relationships are essential during stress management. Spending time with friends and family members and having positive conversations with them can help you distance yourself from the urge to play and focus on the enjoyable aspects of life.

Personal care: It is important to take time for yourself. The body and mind need constant care. Proper sleep, a balanced diet, relaxing baths, therapeutic massage, maintaining rigorous hygiene and regular exercise are essential to maintain emotional balance and reduce stress levels.

Ask for reframing techniques: You can learn to identify negative thoughts and try to replace them with positive comments. If you fail at something, try to pick up an opportunity from that failure and keep trying differently until you succeed.

Adopting a healthy lifestyle A balanced diet, quality sleep and adequate hydration are fundamental to lead a healthy life. Make sure both your body and mind are relaxed. Avoid getting exhausted or overloaded. It is crucial to keep your body and mind in optimal condition

Wisdom: That deep treasure born of deep thoughts and life experiences comes at an immeasurable cost – time. In the hustle and bustle of life, where every minute is counted, we often forget how precious our time is. We are constantly engulfed in everyday life, urgent tasks and the desire for immediate results, ignoring that wisdom does not fit into this hurried pattern.

To cultivate wisdom, I have learned that it is essential to take time to grow, learn from our experiences, meditate on the complexities of life, and evolve personally. It is not a quick fix; It's a lifelong journey.

Every experience, every lesson, and every moment of reflection enriches our wisdom. It is more than just gathering knowledge; It is the ability to apply what we have learned meaningfully to our daily lives. Wisdom guides us in making thoughtful decisions, navigating challenges with serenity, and understanding ourselves and the world around us on a deeper level.

However, like a slow-growing tree, wisdom takes time to develop strong roots. This growth cannot be rushed or achieved by a quick course. It is a natural, gradual process.

This realization makes me appreciate that our time is one of our most precious resources. Devoting time to self-discovery, lifelong learning and personal development is an investment in ourselves. The cost of time is immeasurable, ultimately revealing itself as a priceless gift to ourselves and the world. These are some essential stress management techniques. Try all methods; Some ways will really work for you.

Financial planning

Financial planning is an essential element in the recovery process, helping to overcome gambling addiction. It is important to manage financial matters carefully by creating a list of income and expenses. A balanced budget is the key to financial success. The synergy between motivation and financial resources can be a powerful catalyst for transformative change, especially when directed towards noble societal goals. This combination shows how motivated, adequately funded individuals can make substantial contributions to society. Here are some essential steps in making a financial plan.

Financial Condition Assessment: The first step is to determine your financial strength and list your expenses, liabilities, and income. Knowing your current financial situation can help you make better plans accordingly. Finding out the accepted problem and diagnosing the problem is considered a half-way solution.

Set a budget: Make a budget with the details of your income and expenses. While making a budget and allocating the amount for necessities like bills, food, and rent, remember to give an amount to pay off debts and even some savings or emergency funds. After you make a budget, be disciplined and stick to the budget. You can avoid any risk of falling into new financial dependencies and manage your money effectively.

Debt reduction and elimination: Identify all obligations during financial planning, strategize, and look for sources to phase out debt. Also, avoid new loans; They will be an extra burden for you and you will not be able to free yourself from old debts.

Consult a financial specialist: If you have done all the financial planning and failed to achieve your goals, consult a financial specialist or debt advisor. They can help you formulate professional financial plans and strategies to set a healthy financial path.

Saving and investment planning: Once you've eliminated all loans and debts, you can focus on keeping your assets. Set realistic short-, medium- and long-term goals and set aside an amount of your income for savings and investments. You can open a savings account and invest in mutual funds as well. Currently, online copy trading is the most popular form of investment.

Avoiding financial temptations: A proactive approach is to be aware of the risks of falling into new financial dependencies and to avoid situations that may expose you to temptations. Always stay away from gambling sites and apps. Make well-informed and responsible choices to ensure your financial stability and security.

Continuing financial education: Investing in yourself is considered one of the best forms of investment, so dedicate time and effort to learning and developing your financial skills. You can read books on financial management, attend seminars and webinars on economics, watch YouTube videos about those topics, and take financial courses on Udemy. If you are well informed, you can make the best financial decisions and build a stable financial future. These are some essential suggestions related to financial planning. You should also seek advice tailored to your situation. financial and long-term goals.

Replacing gambling with positive activities

The art of turning threats into opportunities must be learned. How can we turn negative thoughts into positive thoughts? This approach tells you how to engage in healthy, satisfying, joyful activities. Some essential suggestions are outlined below.

Motivated individuals, often driven by passion and vision, have the drive and determination to initiate change and innovate. However, their images may remain unfulfilled dreams without the necessary financial support. Financial resources are essential to turn ideas into reality, enabling well-designed plans to be executed and turning potential into tangible results.

For example, a team motivated to address global environmental issues can, with adequate funding, develop sustainable technologies, contribute to green initiatives, or engage in climate change mitigation efforts. In the field of humanitarian aid, financial resources can amplify the impact of motivated individuals and organisations striving to alleviate suffering and improve living conditions in disadvantaged communities.

Discover and develop new hobbies: Brainstorm and try to discover those activities that inspire you. Make a list of your top ten activities. It could be painting, long car rides, photography, gardening, cooking, writing, reading books, exercising at the gym, traveling, dancing. Choose an activity that piques your curiosity and makes you happy. And make it a regular part of your life.

Engage in physical activity: Exercise can positively affect your mood and health. You can work out at the gym, swim, run, hike, take morning walks, do yoga and dance. Physical movements are useful for relieving stress. You also feel full of energy.

Socialize with friends and family: Spend some time with loved ones. Just discuss common matters to distract from gambling. Positive social interaction matters a lot in the recovery process.

Volunteer with community-based organizations: By dedicating time and resources to supporting community projects and charities, such as helping people affected by floods or storms, you will experience deep inner satisfaction and gain a broader perspective on life. This involvement will give you the opportunity to meet new people and form valuable social bonds.

Develop new skills: Develop skills you like. Dance, graphic design, painting, storytelling and dance. Meet those experts in that skill and learn from them. You can expand your knowledge through online courses.

Explore nature: Nature is like a mother. If you are tired of the boring life of gambling, go hiking, camping or simply walk in a park near nature, you will be mentally relaxed. Connecting to nature has a calming and revitalizing effect on the body and mind.

Read and learn continuously: Reading books opens up new avenues of knowledge. By choosing books of different genres, you will explore new worlds. Your concentration and attention span will also increase along with your comprehension. You can find audiobooks online to learn and discover new things.

Participate in cultural and artistic events: You can participate in art exhibitions or other events in your community. You can visit museums and theaters as they will give you inspiration and connect you to the world of art and culture.

Practice mindfulness and meditation: If you want to calm your mind, practice mindfulness and meditation. These practices will lower your stress levels and make you able to enjoy the present moment.

Join interest groups/hobbies: Consult locally or online those groups that have the same interests and hobbies as you: book clubs, knitting groups, sports teams, or travelers. Try connecting with them.

These are some suggestions for positive activities to replace gaming activities. I recommend exploring these suggestions and getting a benefit from them that is compatible with your needs.

Help from family and friends

The most important resource that can support you in the process of getting out of gambling addiction is family and friends. There are various ways they can offer you help.

Emotional support: They can give you emotional support during difficult times, and when you're in a weak emotional state and in a bad mood, they motivate you. Because they are worried about you, they listen carefully to your problems and worries, then encourage you and give you the courage to fight your problems.

Identify signs of relapse: Family and friends may notice early signs of a possible relapse in addiction because they know you best. Always be open to them, discuss your problems. and ask for their feedback. Working with them, formulate preventive strategies and measures that are useful for you to maintain your abstinence.

Participate in therapy and support groups: You can involve one of your best friends or family. They can learn how to better help you and understand your challenges. They may attend family therapy sessions to develop a standard recovery plan.

Creating a safe and temptation-free environment: Friends and family members can create an environment where there are no temptations to play. They can remove access to gambling sites, restrict access to money to be used for gambling, and remove anything that reminds you of gambling.

Engaging in healthy joint activities: Friends and family members can be involved in healthy activities with you, planning trips together, going to the cinema, or attending any sporting event. These activities not only help you stay connected, but also have healthy fun.

Encouragement and support in recovery plans: A free and constant source of involvement and support is always with you, in the form of family and friends. Communicate openly about your goals, progress and problems; They will assist, motivate and help you in every possible way to quit gambling.

Respecting your limits and decisions: Once you have identified your limits and made decisions, share them with family and friends, and they will respect your limits and gambling decisions. Tell them what you expect from them and then they will definitely help you. Give them confidence and guide them to respect your choices.

Remember, the most important thing is trust in relationships, so never lose trust and always be open to friends and family members. Their mutual support is essential in the process of quitting gambling. Appreciate them and be grateful for their unconditional help and support throughout your recovery journey.

Gaming Industry: From Beginnings to a Global Phenomenon

The story of the gaming industry from the early 1900s to 2023 is a gripping saga of transformation, reflecting changes in society and technological leaps. Let's explore this journey.

1900s: First Days in the Shadows

In the 1900s, gambling was secret and hidden. Think hidden horse racing, secret card games and gambling machines hidden in silence.

1950s: The emergence of legal gambling and casino culture

Year 1950. A turning point came with the legalization of gambling in places like Nevada. Las Vegas began its rise to fame, marking the era with newfound legitimacy. Although the industry's revenues were only a trickle compared to future figures, they were significant enough to set the stage for what was to come.

2000s: Online Revolution

In the early 2000s, online gambling emerged and changed everything. By 2005, their value was around $12 billion, shaking up the industry and bringing in many new players because it was so easy to access.

2023: A mastodon of entertainment

In 2023, the industry exploded and turned into a staggering enterprise of over $500 billion. Relentless technological advances, mobile gambling and an ever-expanding legal landscape have fueled this explosive growth.

Mobile gambling wave

In the 2010s, smartphones became a game changer. By 2023, mobile gambling accounted for a massive slice of the online gambling pie, with more than half of all online bets being placed on mobile devices.

Advertising: The Hidden Engine of Industry

Gambling advertising has seen a spectacular evolution. From the early 2000s, when hundreds of millions of euros were invested in advertising, to 2023, the industry is escalating to billions of dollars in marketing. These impressive sums are directed towards digital platforms, television and sports sponsorships, reflecting a radical transformation in the way the industry is promoted.

Societal impact and call for regulation

This explosive growth has not been a challenge. Concerns about gambling addiction have led to stricter regulations. For example, the UK Gambling Commission, established in 2005, set out to impose responsible gambling.

Looking to the future

In the future, the gaming industry will continue to develop, with innovations such as virtual reality and blockchain opening up new horizons. However, this increase is likely to be accompanied by a stronger push for ethical practices and stricter regulations.

Reflect on a century of change

The evolution of the gaming industry, from a covert operation in the 1900s to a global power in 2023, mirrors broader societal changes and technological leaps. As the industry moves into the future, it faces the ongoing challenge of balancing economic success with social responsibility and regulatory compliance.

Blocking access to gambling/gambling sites

Now, I share with you a comprehensive list of 100 methods that will help you quit gambling. Many of these are based on my personal experiences, so I suggest you explore these methods. These methods have the potential to help; You can try them all and find the most effective one.

"Success comes from doing extraordinary ordinary things." – Jim Rohn

List of 100 methods to block access to gambling:

1. Install gambling blocking apps: Download and use apps designed to block access to gambling sites on your smartphones, tablets or computers.

2. Use web filters: Use web content filtering programs or browser extensions to restrict access to gambling sites.

3. Block service providers: Contact your internet service provider and ask them to block access to gambling sites.

4. Secure passwords: Create strong and unique passwords for all gambling-related accounts and ensure they are stored securely.

5. Self-exclusion: Sign up for self-exclusion programs offered by casinos and gambling sites to voluntarily ban yourself from their services.

6. Family assistance: Involve your friends and family in your support by helping you block access to gambling sites.

7. Online payment limits: Set limits on your methods. online payment, making it difficult to deposit funds for gambling.

8. Secure payment cards: Store your credit and debit cards securely to reduce impulsive gambling.

9. Blocking bank transactions: Contact your bank or financial institution to request that gambling-related transactions be blocked.

10. Alternative activities: Find hobbies and interests outside of gambling, such as sports, reading, or gardening, to occupy your time.

11. Avoid triggering: Recognize and avoid situations or environments that trigger the urge to play.

12. Social circle: Avoid spending time with people who engage in or promote gambling activities.

13. Device usage limits: Set time limits for your devices. electronics, especially in times of vulnerability.

14. Time management: Organize your daily schedule effectively to reduce downtime that could lead to gambling.

15. Resource research: Explore offline and online resources that provide guidance and support for overcoming gambling addiction.

16. Social engagement: Attend social events and activities to distract yourself from gambling.

17. Remove game objects: Remove from your environment. any physical objects or reminders associated with gambling.

18. Creative pursuits: Engage in creative hobbies and community service to channel your energy positively.

19. Goal setting: Set short, medium, and long-term goals to guide and motivate your recovery.

20. Emotional support: Rely on the emotional support of loved ones who can give you encouragement and motivation.

21. Online Support Groups: Join online communities and support groups to connect with others facing similar challenges.

22. Remember the damage: Always remind yourself of the negative consequences and harm caused by gambling.

23. Professional help: Seek assistance from therapists and support groups specializing in addiction recovery.

24. Notification control: Turn off notifications from gambling-related apps or websites to reduce temptation.

25. New hobbies: Discover and engage in new hobbies and interests to occupy your mind and time.

26. Entertainment limits: Set strict limits on the time and money you spend on entertainment.

27. Recreation: Participate in recreational activities not related to gambling.

28. Daily Diary: Keep a daily journal to record your thoughts, emotions, and progress on your recovery journey.

29. Highlights: Break down your recovery into achievable milestones, celebrating each step forward.

30. Learn from others: Seek advice and insights from people who have successfully overcome gambling addiction.

31. Help the community: Contact non-governmental organizations (NGOs) and local communities for additional support.

32. Personal development: Participate in individual development programs and workshops to improve various aspects of your life.

33. Online forums: Participate in online forums where you can share your experiences and ask others for advice.

34. Support network: Use your social network of friends, family, and colleagues for emotional support.

35. Self-hypnosis: Explore self-hypnosis techniques for relaxation and stress management.

36. Trigger Plan: Develop a plan to identify and manage situations or triggers that lead to gambling.

37. Time management tools: Use online time management templates and tools to efficiently organize your daily activities.

38. Financial seminars: Attend seminars and workshops focused on financial management to gain control over your finances.

39. Avoid gambling locations: Avoid places or locations associated with gambling activities.

40. Review spending: Regularly evaluate your expenses to identify and reduce unnecessary spending.

41. Self-rewards: Establish a self-reward system for achieving specific milestones in the recovery process.

42. Avoid alcohol/substances: Avoid alcohol or substances that can lower inhibitions and lead to impulsive gambling.

43. Motivational videos: Watch motivational videos to stay inspired and motivated on your recovery journey.

44. Conflict resolution: Learn effective conflict resolution techniques to manage interpersonal challenges.

45. Physical activity: Prioritize physical activity and exercise to improve your physical and mental well-being.

46. Reading: Read: Spend time reading in libraries or at home to broaden your knowledge and interests.

47. Positive influence: Surround yourself with positive people who uplift and encourage you.

48. Communication skills: Develop strong communication skills to effectively manage conflicts and relationships.

49. Relaxation breaks: Take breaks and find moments of mental relaxation to reduce stress.

50. Leisure planning: Plan your free time carefully to ensure it promotes relaxation and positivity.

51. List your interests: Create a list of your passions and interests. to explore them at your leisure.

52. Success stories: Find inspiration and motivation by reading success stories of people who have overcome addiction.

53. Personal commitment: Make a firm and unwavering commitment to quit gambling.

54. Stay busy: Keep yourself busy and involved to prevent game thoughts from recurring.

55. Relax music: Relax: Listen to soothing music to relax and reduce stress.

56. Find a mentor: Seek guidance, advice, and motivation from a mentor who can support your journey.

57. Self-motivation: Practice self-motivation and cultivate a positive mindset to stay on track.

58. Motivational films: Watch movies and documentaries that inspire and encourage positive change.

59. Positive conversations: Engage in conversations about positivity, growth, and well-being.

60. Pet companion: Consider adopting a pet to provide companionship and responsibility.

61. Savings jar: Use a savings jar to visually represent your progress and financial goals.

62. Optimistic mindset: Maintain a bright and hopeful outlook on your journey to recovery.

63. Motivational courses: Invest in courses and programs that provide additional motivation and guidance.

64. Alternative Games: Play video games without gambling or engage in recreational activities that do not involve gambling.

65. Think about solutions: Think and implement effective strategies for managing addiction and cravings.

66. Storytelling workshops: Participate in storytelling workshops to creatively express your experiences and emotions.

67. Distraction-free workspace: Create a focused, distraction-free work environment to boost productivity.

68. Visualize success: Practice visualization techniques to imagine a future without gambling addiction.

69. Defying your comfort zone: Step out of your comfort zone and embrace new experiences and challenges.

70. Adjusting goals: Adjust your goals to adapt to changing circumstances and progress.

71. Practice mindfulness and stay present in the moment to reduce stress and anxiety.

72. Self-pity: Be kind and compassionate toward yourself. especially during recessions.

73. Change your environment: Consider changing your physical environment if it supports your recovery.

74. Focus on control: Focus on aspects of your life. that you can control to maintain a sense of agency.

75. Learn from mistakes: Learn from any ineffective recovery methods or past mistakes to improve your approach.

76. Patience: Show patience as you progress on your recovery journey, recognizing that change takes time.

77. Self-confidence: Develop confidence in overcoming gambling addiction and making positive choices.

78. Learn from relapses: Gain insights from any relapses and use it as opportunities for growth and improvement.

79. Plan for boredom: Plan for moments of boredom to make sure you have constructive activities to occupy your time.

80. Revive hobbies: Rediscover and revive old hobbies and interests that you may have neglected during addiction.

81. Special Event Alertness: Exercise vigilance and caution during special events or occasions that may trigger game impulses.

82. Resolve stress: Develop effective strategies to cope with stress and manage life's challenges without resorting to gambling.

83. Remember the losses: Remember the financial and personal losses that gambling can bring.

84. Identify self-sabotage: Recognize and address self-sabotaging behaviors that hinder your progress.

85. Gratitude list: Create a daily gratitude list to encourage a positive and appreciative mindset.

86. Multifaceted approach: Implement a combination of various methods and strategies to increase the effectiveness of your recovery.

Using time management techniques, you can devise a plan, add more productive activities, and aim for a victory. These are the various methods that can definitely help you block access to gambling and ultimately lead to rebuilding your life. in a balanced and healthy way. Since each person is unique, just like their circumstances, you need to try all methods and choose the ones that best suit your situation and bring positive results.

Bets Against the Odds: The 10 Captivating Stories of Gamblers

Next, I will share the stories of some bettors who have gone through difficult times. Some gave up and lost their fortune, while few had the courage to fight gambling addiction and celebrate victory.

Beyond the glamour of casinos: Stories of defeat

One hand

Daniel, a brilliant MBA graduate, gets a job as a cashier at a bank, a role that seemed to secure him a stable future. His family, including his younger brother John, who was juggling law school studies and a part-time job, relied on him for guidance. The sudden death of their father forced Daniel and John to take on the role of caregivers for the family, a responsibility they both took seriously.

Daniel's fall into gambling addiction began almost unnoticed. It started as a harmless way to escape work stress and family responsibilities. The first gains were exciting, giving him a seemingly quick path to the financial security he wanted. But as the stakes went up, so did his gambling addiction.

John, preoccupied with his own life, hadn't noticed the seriousness of Daniel's growing addiction until it was too late. By then, Daniel had begun to believe that gambling could be the solution to his financial problems.

The decisive moment came when Daniel bet everything in a poker game, building on previous successes. The loss was devastating, wiping out all his savings and pushing him into an abyss of debt. His performance at work declined, eventually leading to his dismissal from the bank. With huge debts and his brother also trapped in gambling addiction, Daniel's life began to fall apart.

With bills rising and debts spiraling out of control, Daniel's family struggled to stay afloat. He started selling goods and borrowing money, but it was never enough. The financial crisis put enormous pressure on his marriage. His wife, overwhelmed by stress and social stigma, decided to leave with their children to her parents.

This situation was a wake-up call for Daniel. Realizing the damage his gambling addiction had caused, he decided to seek help. She sought out a therapist who specialized in addictions and together they developed a recovery plan.

The road to recovery was long and full of obstacles, but Daniel was determined to succeed. He found a new job, although it was paid less than the previous one, and began to rebuild his life step by step. Paying off debts and repairing relationships became his main goals.

Daniel's story is a sober reminder of the dangers of gambling addiction and the importance of facing life's challenges. It is a story of fall and recovery, proving that with determination, support and professional assistance, it is possible to overcome even the deepest struggles.

Spoiled dreams

Cristina, a dedicated academic studying abroad on a scholarship, never imagined that poker would become more than just fun with friends. It all started quite simply, a suggestion from a friend to play a few hands after exams. Initially, it was a thrilling way to relax and unwind. The small victories were exhilarating, giving Cristina a sense of easy achievement.

However, her situation changed drastically after a minor accident landed her in hospital. Medical bills quickly depleted his limited savings. Coming from a low-income background, Cristina has always been careful about her finances, but this unexpected expense hit her hard. She is in a desperate situation, with exam fees in full swing and savings almost exhausted.

In a moment of panic and necessity, Cristina gambled up her remaining savings, hoping to earn enough to cover her academic expenses. It was a gamble driven by despair, not desire. The night she entered the casino, Cristina carried not only dwindling funds, but also a heavy heart, burdened by fear of the consequences of her actions.

As it turned out, luck wasn't on Christina's side that night. With each game, her savings escaped, leaving her with nothing. The awareness of his loss was overwhelming. It wasn't just about money — the potential loss of scholarship, education, and all the advances he'd worked so hard for.

Back in her home, the gravity of her situation hit Cristina in full force. He admitted the magnitude of his mistake. There were other ways she could get by—part-time jobs, seeking help, but she had chosen gambling, a shortcut that now seemed so wrong.

Faced with the harsh reality of the consequences of her actions, Cristina is faced with the decision to return home without completing her studies. The dreams she had cultivated through years of hard work and dedication now seemed to disintegrate right before her gaze.

As she began packing her belongings, Cristina reflected on her journey. The lesson was painfully clear: success doesn't come from shortcuts. The attraction of quick wins through gambling led to a significant loss. But in this moment of despair, Cristina knew she had to find the strength to move forward. This was not the end of her story, but a challenging chapter from which she had to learn. With renewed determination and a clearer understanding of the value of hard work and perseverance, Cristina was determined to rebuild her life step by step, learning from the past and focusing on the future.

Total control over everything, or is it just an illusion!

Oliver, 58, had been involved in the gambling scene for five years. During the day, he ran his small shop, a modest but stable source of income. However, as the sun set, he was lured by the bright light of the casino. Oliver believed strongly in overcoming the odds through careful calculations and strategies. This belief in his gambling acumen became his shield against doubt, justifying every bet he made.

Over the years, Oliver built up his confidence in his skills as a player, ignoring an uncomfortable truth: his losses consistently outweighed his gains. The harsh reality of his financial situation became apparent when he had to face the maturity of pawned gold, taken five years ago. The moment he sat down to reconcile his accounts, Oliver was confronted with the harsh truth: gambling had caused him a significant net loss.

This revelation was a harsh awakening for Oliver. He realized that the sense of control he thought he had over gambling was an illusion. But by then, the habit of betting had become deeply ingrained. Despite his age and the visible fatigue creeping into his bones, giving up seemed impossible. The casino had become a part of his routine, a regular quest for the big win that he hoped would change everything.

The repercussions of Oliver's gambling were not limited to him. As head of the family, his actions jeopardized the financial stability of the family. The fear of losing his home because of the unpaid loan and becoming a source of shame for his children weighed heavily on him.

Every night at the casino, Oliver pursued the dream of a big win, a chance to undo losses and start over. But the reality of gambling was harsh; The odds were never really in his favor. Deep down, he knew this, but the charm of the game kept him coming back.

Full of regrets and facing an uncertain future, Oliver's story is a touching example of his devastating gambling addiction. His journey highlights the critical need for awareness and intervention, especially for older adults caught up in gambling. It serves as a stark reminder of the importance of seeking help and breaking free from the destructive cycle of addiction before it's too late.

Gambling

Marius was a middle-class nurse who worked tirelessly to support his family, including his retired father. His life took an unexpected turn when a colleague introduced him to online gambling. What started as an occasional pastime to relax from stress at work soon turned into an obsession. The thrill of winning captivated Marius, leading him to believe that gambling might be an easier way to earn money than his demanding career as a nurse.

Overwhelmed by the charm of quick earnings, Marius quit his stable job as a nurse under the pretext of earning money by freelancing. In reality, he is immersing himself even more in the world of online gambling. Initially, earnings seemed significant, sometimes equating to a month's salary in one day. This success led him to frequent casinos in search of even greater sensations. However, the unpredictable nature of gambling quickly caught on with Marius. His lucky fortune turned into a series of losses, and the money he had earned was quickly depleted by his increased spending on luxury and entertainment. Walking the streets, Marius was haunted by a tumult of regret and anger for his choices. He longed to remake his decisions and put his life on a better path.

The consequences of his gambling were not only financial. Marius had lost his job and was losing hope. His personal life had also suffered; His girlfriend, seeing him struggling, urged him to seek help. She attended therapy sessions and received expert advice, but the grip of her gambling addiction was too firm. Despite his girlfriend's support and efforts to keep him away from gambling, addiction continued to control his life, putting their relationship to the test.

Marius' story is a stark reminder of the dangers of gambling addiction. His journey shows the challenges of breaking deep-rooted habits, highlighting the need for professional support and help. Now, Marius is at a crossroads, his future depending on his ability to overcome the addiction that has taken away so much.

His story highlights the risks associated with gambling and the potential for recovery with the right determination and support. Marius' path to recovery is uncertain, but he is a powerful example of hope that change is possible.

Desperation to win everything: risking losing everything

Peter, a banker by profession and father of three, has always led a life marked by responsibility and stability. However, his world took a drastic turn when, one unfortunate day, he came across an online gambling game. It all started with a simple click on a pop-up notification and a subsequent win that seemed too easy. The congratulatory message on winning $10 and transferring directly to his virtual wallet sparked something in Peter. It seemed like a fun and effortless way to earn some extra money.

With increasing interest, Peter visited the gambling site again the next day. Even the low stakes were exciting, and the thrill of winning and playing was very appealing. Seduced by this new way of making money, he decided to invest more time and resources in the gambling site, believing that it would be profitable. Thus, gambling became a constant part of his daily routine, alternating between wins and losses, but always with the hope of a big jackpot. Life, however, had other plans. A transfer of service required Peter and his family to move to a new city. This change brings financial pressures he had not anticipated, higher living costs and unexpected expenses related to the move. Faced with this new financial burden, Peter saw gambling not only as a hobby, but also as a potential solution to his problems. He started playing harder, hoping to earn enough to cover his expansion expenses.

This decision marked the beginning of a downward spiral. Peter's gambling sessions became longer and more frequent, consuming up to 20-22 hours over several days each week. This obsessive gambling began to overshadow everything else: his family, his social life, and even his health. His sleep patterns were disrupted and soon his physical well-being began to deteriorate, leading to high blood pressure and diabetes.

At home, tensions were rising. His wife continually expresses concern about Peter's unbalanced lifestyle and his growing obsession with online gambling. She warned him of the risks and consequences he was having on their family life. But Peter, consumed by the gambling world, ignores her concerns. He was convinced that a big win was just around the corner, a win that would solve all their problems.

The reality, however, was far from his expectations. The more he gambled, the more distant his family became. They couldn't stand by and watch Peter put everything on the line for gambling. His health continued to deteriorate and pressure on his relationships increased.

In a moment of introspection, Peter realized the gravity of his situation. He reflected on his choices, acknowledging opportunities he had missed to secure his family's future through more prudent financial decisions. The regret of not having saved or invested with wisdom weighed heavily on him. He understood that the root cause of his current situation was gambling addiction and that breaking this cycle was essential to change the trajectory of his life.

Alone and confronted with his choices, Peter understood that the road to recovery would be difficult. He had to muster the courage, determination, and motivation to overcome his addiction. His once-bright and promising future now depended on his ability to make meaningful changes.

Peter's story serves as a powerful lesson about the dangers of gambling addiction. She highlights the importance of seeking help and making responsible life choices, demonstrating that the attraction of quick money can have devastating long-term consequences. Although fraught with difficulties, his journey also offers hope – that it's never too late to change things and start over.

Overcoming Gambling: The Stories of Those Who Left This Addiction Behind

Here are five inspirational stories of winners who never gave up fighting gambling addiction. How did they manage to triumph? We will explore these cases in detail further.

The story of 2 brothers

The story of Ben and Mark, two brothers trapped in gambling addiction, reveals a compelling narrative of divergent paths stemming from shared beginnings. Ben, the older of the two, was deeply involved in gambling. His addiction began to dominate every aspect of his life, overshadowing his family responsibilities and affecting his health and career. Despite several attempts, Ben had had difficulty freeing himself from the clutches of gambling, entering a gradual but inexorable decline.

Mark, influenced by his older brother, also started acting. However, by observing Ben's ongoing struggle with addiction, Mark gained a crucial awareness. At the age of 40, Mark realized he was at a crossroads; He could either continue down this destructive path or make a major change. He chose to change his life.

Retreating to a quiet place, Mark sought clarity and a fresh start. There he created a detailed plan to overcome gambling addiction. He dedicated himself to the study of various resources to give up games and strategies for personal success. Determined to replace destructive habits with positive efforts, Mark embarked on the world of freelancing. His initial, modest successes were an important step in his transformation.

The next leg of Mark's journey brought him to a picturesque region full of hills, a place he has always felt connected to. This environmental change played a crucial role in his recovery. Inspired by the surrounding landscape, Mark started creating vlogs, capturing the essence of mountains, lakes and waterfalls. Although his YouTube channel initially struggled, Mark remained focused on his main goal: excellence in freelancing.

A year into his freelance career, Mark has reaped the fruits of his perseverance. By becoming a top freelancer, he managed to gain recognition for his hard work, becoming a symbol of his triumph over gambling addiction. In addition to his professional success, Mark enriched his life with physical activities, including morning walks in the mountains, which significantly improved his overall health and well-being.

Mark's success in freelancing not only freed him from his gambling addiction, but also paved the way for his financial recovery. He paid off his debts and rediscovered his passion for vlogging, which now serves as a source of mental refreshment and a means to share the beauty of his new medium.

In contrast to Ben, whose struggles with gambling persisted, Mark became a symbol of hope and positive change in his family and community. His journey from the depths of addiction to success in freelancing and beyond became an inspirational story, often invoked by relatives and friends as an outstanding example of life transformation.

Ben and Mark's stories illustrate the profound impact of our choices on life. Faced with similar challenges, their divergent paths emphasize the strength of determination and the possibility of redemption. Mark's decision to embrace change and pursue personal growth not only freed him from addiction, but also led him to a life of success and fulfillment.

Overcoming Addiction: Gabriel's Transformation Story

Gabriel's story is a moving account of struggle, redemption and transformation, marking his journey from the depths of gambling addiction to a life full of purpose and dedicated to helping others. A successful former banker, Gabriel's foray into gambling began harmlessly, but quickly intensified to dominate his life. This dangerous habit has led him down a path that threatens both his financial stability and moral values. In a desperate attempt to sustain his addiction, Gabriel resorted to stealing money from his brother-in-law, an act that deeply conflicted with his values and integrity.

Realizing the destructive impact of his actions not only on himself, but also on his loved ones, was the moment of awakening for Gabriel. This motivated him to seek change. She sought professional help and found a therapist who specialized in gambling addiction. Together they developed a plan for addressing his addiction, establishing steps and strategies to prevent relapse.

Gabriel also got involved in support groups, where he found solidarity and understanding among others with similar struggles. This community became a source of strength and encouragement, helping him navigate the difficult road of recovery.

An important part of his healing process was adopting new healthy routines. Gabriel began taking regular morning walks in the park, using this time for reflection and distance from the temptations of gambling. He carefully assessed his finances, setting strict budgets and prioritizing debt repayment.

Exploring a creative outing, Gabriel turned to writing, channeling his experiences and insights into a book he self-publishes on Amazon Kindle Direct Publishing. The sale of his first book was a decisive moment, strengthening his confidence in his ability to change and giving him a new direction, away from gambling. Along his journey, Gabriel achieved a remarkable achievement – quitting casinos altogether and freeing himself from the chains of gambling addiction. This victory signified a new beginning in his life.

But Gabriel's transformation didn't stop at his own recovery. He felt an urge to try to help others struggling with gambling addiction. By sharing his story and lessons learned, he became a beacon of hope, supporting and guiding those in need. Gabriel's story demonstrates the power of resilience and the human capacity for radical change. It illustrates the importance of acknowledging mistakes, seeking help, and taking decisive steps toward recovery. His journey from addiction to becoming an example for his community underlines that with determination, support and renewed purpose, it is possible to transform your life and have a positive impact on others.

The Road from Dependency to Renewal and Contribution

Alexander's story and his struggle with gambling addiction is a moving one of transformation and redemption, marking his journey from the depths of addiction to a life with a clear purpose and dedicated to helping others. Once a successful banker, Alexander's slide into gambling began innocently, but quickly degenerated. The lure of the game and the prospect of winning began to dominate his life, leading him down a dangerous path that endangered his financial stability and moral values. In a desperate move to support gambling, he stole money from a family member, a decision that later filled him with remorse and shame.

Alexander's family intervened, recognizing the destructive path their son was on. His father took the drastic but necessary step of blocking his access to both bank accounts and gambling sites. Deprived of access to his addiction, Alexandru entered a state of agitation, facing stress and depression resulting from lack of gambling, which led to tensions in family relationships.

The moment of change for Alexander came after he endured much suffering and realized the need to free himself from this addiction. With the help of professional counseling, she began to take small but significant steps toward recovery. An initial strategy for overcoming addiction was to engage in travel. Planning trips with friends gives him a necessary fun and relaxation, helping him calm his mind. She also found solace in reconnecting with family and friends, using these interactions to share her experiences.

In addition, Alexander began to walk in the park in the morning, using the time for reflection and distance from temptations. He began to read more, strengthening his mind and expanding his knowledge. These positive activities led to significant changes in his lifestyle and mindset. Alexandru created an environment conducive to recovery, surrounding himself with supportive people and adopting healthy habits. Through these efforts, he rediscovered his inner strength to quit gambling and began a new life.

Alexander's recovery is an impressive example of the human capacity to radically change life. His story is a reminder of the power of second chances and the importance of proper support and a positive mindset in overcoming addiction

George's Journey to Recovery and Self-Discovery

The story of George, a talented young man from Greece, is a compelling example of the power of change and the resilience of the human spirit. Coming from a middle-class family, George was drawn into the seductive world of gambling, believing it to be a way to support his family financially. However, the path he chose quickly led him to addiction, causing more harm than good.

George's life came to a turning point when he was caught playing illegally, a serious crime in Greece. The consequences of this arrest - social shame and disappointment of his family - affected him deeply, especially his father. That night was filled with remorse and dark thoughts for George, realizing the mistakes he had made.

The crucial moment of change came when George honestly confronted his father, promising him that he would quit gambling and make him proud. This promise was the beginning of a profound transformation. George left his hometown and moved to a new city, seeking to escape the shadows of his past.

In his new home, George discovered an art workshop that became his sanctuary and the source of his transformation. He began to paint, finding solace and expression through art. His works, inspired by the beauty of nature, were not just paintings; They were illustrations of his inner journey, turning his struggles into visual art.

By participating in an international art competition, George exhibited his works and, to his surprise, won. This success was more than an artistic achievement; It was a validation of his new direction in life.

Motivated by this triumph, George continued to devote himself to art, gradually building a reputation and managing to move to Australia with his family. The reunion with his father was a triumphant moment, reflecting the promise fulfilled and the new life he had built.

George became not only an acclaimed artist, but also an inspiration to his community. His experience culminated in writing a book, a story about his struggles and victories designed to inspire and guide others. Through this book, George demonstrated that redirecting energies from destructive habits to creative passions can lead to deep personal growth and success.

His story is a reminder that, regardless of life's challenges, overcoming them and emerging victorious is possible through courage, determination and a creative channel of expression.

Alexander's Renaissance: From Obscurity to Light

The story of Radu, raised in a modest family in a small village in Bulgaria, is a testimony to the power of transformation and human resilience. Radu's childhood was marked by difficulties and deprivation, but also by a burning desire to overcome his condition. Reaching adulthood, Radu was attracted to the world of entrepreneurship, seeing it as a way to change his destiny and help his family. Despite his enthusiasm and ambition, his path was full of obstacles and failures. Looking for a quick solution to his financial problems, Radu started playing the lottery, hoping for a miraculous change of fate. However, this harmless habit turned into an addiction, which began to consume both his finances and mood.

Disappointment and shame peaked when he lost a large amount of money, which caused Radu to reevaluate his life. This painful experience was the turning point in his life. Determined to change his destiny, Radu gave up gambling and channeled his energy towards self-development.

He started by redefining his goals and developing his business skills. She enrolled in online courses, read personal development and business books, and began attending entrepreneurship seminars and conferences. In the process, Radu discovered his passion for technology and innovation.

With his new vision, Radu launched a technology start-up. The road was not easy, but determination and self-confidence helped him overcome many challenges.
This start-up began to take shape, attracting the attention of investors, which led to its gradual success. This success not only

changed Radu's life, but also had a positive impact on his community. By investing in local projects and providing jobs to talented young people in his village, he thus contributed to the economic development of the area.

Radu's story is an inspiration for all those who face challenges and obstacles. It demonstrates that with willpower and hard work, it is possible to turn a difficult situation into a success story. His journey from gambling addiction to successful entrepreneur illustrates how perseverance and self-development can pave the way to remarkable achievement and positive impact in the community.

The Science of Addiction

"Gambling addiction, like cancer, is a condition that cannot be completely cured, but can be meticulously managed and kept under control." Ciprian Ipate

Just like cancer, gambling addiction can subtly invade various aspects of an individual's life, often going unnoticed at first. It usually starts with occasional bets or occasional visits to the casino. However, over time, this habit can grow and permeate aspects such as personal relationships, financial stability, and mental health. Early detection helps manage gambling addiction, just as early detection for cancer is important. The longer the habit remains unrecognized or unaddressed, the more ingrained it becomes, making the road to recovery increasingly difficult. Recognizing the problem, often shrouded in denial, is an essential first step, akin to accepting a cancer diagnosis.

The journey with gambling addiction is less about searching for a cure and more about effective management and treatment. This process often involves therapy, support groups, lifestyle adjustments, and sometimes medications, mirroring cancer treatments that aim to control the disease and improve quality of life. Relapse in managing gambling addiction is akin to remission and recurrence of cancer. It's not a sign of failure, but a natural part of recovery. Each regression provides lessons and perspectives, contributing to a deeper understanding of triggers and coping strategies.

Just as cancer patients rely on health professionals, family, and friends, people struggling with gambling addiction need a solid support system. This network often includes addiction therapists, support groups such as Gamblers Anonymous, as well as empathetic family members and friends who provide both emotional and practical support. Managing gambling addiction also requires continuous effort and significant lifestyle changes.

It involves creating an environment that reduces temptations and prioritizes healthy, satisfying activities, similar to lifestyle changes recommended for cancer patients.

The comparison between gambling addiction and cancer highlights the severity, need for ongoing management and multifaceted approach needed to live with this challenge. It serves as a reminder that although a straightforward cure can be elusive, there is hope and potential for effective management and control of gambling addiction, leading to a balanced and rewarding life.

Physical aspects of gambling addiction

Gambling addiction is also called pathological gambling or gambling disorder. It's an uncontrollable behavioral need to play. Psychologically, it looks very familiar with abuse disorder, including the development of tolerance, withdrawal symptoms and activation of the brain's reward mechanisms systems.

A few basic factors are.

The illusion of control: Players believe they have total control over the game; Instead, it's a game of chance.

Cognitive distortions: These are misconceptions about gambling, such as gambler bankruptcy, according to which a gain is due after a few losses.

Reinforcement programs: The unpredictable nature of gambling can create a reinforcement program, similar to variable ratio reinforcement in psychology.

Neurological aspects of gambling addiction

Neurologically, gambling addiction affects the brain's reward system; It deregulates it. During gambling, the brain releases dopamine. It is a neurotransmitter directly associated with reward and pleasure, a feeling called euphoria, "high." Over time, the brain's neural system has altered, leading to:

Desensitization: As the brain is addicted to high levels of emotion, it needs more gambling and risk-taking to maintain the same level of excitement and excitement.

Altered decision-making: Gambling addiction affects the prefrontal cortex, which affects a person's ability to make rational decisions and resist impulses.

Withdrawal systems: Because the brain has become accustomed to high levels of dopamine, sudden reductions in gambling activities can lead to withdrawal symptoms.

False evidence that seems real

Its abbreviation as FEAR (False Evidence Appearing Real) encapsulates very well how our perceptions can often mislead us, especially regarding our anxiety and decisions. This concept is incredibly insightful in understanding the psychological underpinnings of challenges such as addictions, phobias, and daily worries. Fear is essentially a trick of the mind that convinces us of dangers that may not exist. It is when we perceive a situation as threatening or harmful, despite evidence to the contrary. This distorted perception can lead to anxiety and panic, clouding our ability to see things as they are.

In our daily lives, fear can take many forms. It can be the fear of failure that prevents us from trying new endeavors, the fear of rejection that prevents us from expressing our true feelings, or the fear of being judged that prevents us from showing our true identity. Often at the root of these fears is not present reality, but assumptions, past experiences or misunderstandings.

Fear can be a significant, albeit negative, influence when making decisions. It can lead to postponing important tasks, avoiding challenges, or making choices that are not in our best interest. Decisions made under the influence of fear often prevent us from realizing our full potential and growing as individuals.
To combat fear, developing self-awareness and engaging in critical thinking is essential. This means questioning the truth behind our fears and challenging the evidence to support them. Approaches such as cognitive-behavioral therapy (CBT) can be particularly effective in identifying and reinterpreting irrational fears.

In the influence of addiction such as gambling addiction, fear often plays a critical role. This can manifest as fear of losing a coping mechanism, fear of facing life's challenges without vice, or fear of stigma associated with seeking help. Understanding and addressing these fears is helpful on the journey to recovery because it often involves realizing that these fears are based more on misconceptions or exaggerated threats than reality. There are practical steps one can take to overcome fear:

1. **Identify fear**: Make it clear what you are afraid of. Is it a specific situation, a potential outcome, or something else entirely?
2. **Challenge her reality**: Examine the evidence for and against your fear. How likely is it that what you fear will happen?
3. **Look for alternative perspectives**: Talk to other people or seek professional guidance for getting different views on your fear.
4. **Develop coping skills**: Learn techniques to manage anxiety and stress more effectively.
5. **Take gradual steps**: Slowly expose yourself to the source of your fear in a controlled way, gaining confidence over time.

Recognizing fear as "False evidence that seems real" provides a powerful insight into mental and emotional well-being. It urges us to examine our fears, understand their origins, and work to overcome them. By doing so, we open ourselves up to new experiences, a deeper understanding, and a greater awareness of our potential and capabilities.

Gambling Addiction: The Influence of Culture and Social Environment

Society/culture and the environment can also have an impact on an individual's behaviors, such as gambling addiction. For example, if a person lives in a society where gambling is considered very bad for their cultural norms, then this has a harsh impact on individual behavior. If it is a person addicted to gambling in a community where people understand the nature, dynamics and causes of his addiction, they show sympathy for him and try to help him get out of this situation; He doesn't leave her alone. Because leaving them alone on their own can lead to disaster.

Replacing gambling-induced euphoria with beneficial and constructive activities

With the help of various positive activities and alternative sources of pleasure, it is the best way to cope with gambling-related disorders. These activities stimulate the release of neurotransmitters like dopamine, serotonin, and endorphins, which regulate your mood and give you a sense of well-being.

Neuroplasticity is fundamental, the brain's ability to form a new neural connection for recognition. Scientific research has proven that people can rewrite their brains to find pleasure by engaging in positive activities. There are various positive activities through which we can promote our well-being, rather than destructive behaviors. A few of them are mentioned below.

Hobbies and skill development: Activities such as learning musical instruments, painting or playing football/cricket can boost the brain's healthy reward system.

Exercise: Regular exercise has been shown to produce endorphins and dopamine to improve mood and reduce stress levels.

Social connections: By connecting socially with other people, the brain releases oxytocin which promotes bonding and reduces stress levels.

Mindfulness and meditation: Another neurotransmitter, serotonin, is triggered by meditation and helps maintain happiness.

Achievements: Achieving goals provides a sense of accomplishment, stimulating the brain's reward system.

By constantly engaging in positive activities, the brain begins to associate these healthy behaviors with pleasure and reward. Over time, the urge to play reduces and can be part of the recovery process. It is a journey that reduces play habits and cultivates a fulfilling and balanced lifestyle.

Gambling Addiction: Legal and Social Consequences

There are several legal issues related to gambling, such as debt challenges and criminal activities. So it's essential to understand these issues and manage these legal challenges, which is helpful for recovery. These challenges will be discussed in detail below.

Debt and bankruptcy: Gambling not only leads to significant financial stress, but also severely affects the player's ability to pay debts. It is essential to seek legal advice to understand their options, such as debt restructuring, declaring bankruptcy.

Fraud and theft: Sometimes desperation to gamble drives gamblers to commit fraud or theft. Depending on the nature of the crime, consequences include fines and incarceration. Rehabilitation programs and legal defense strategies are considered the best mitigation options.

Family and domestic problems: Gambling not only inversely affects your financial situation, but also affects relationships, such as divorce and child custody disputes. In such scenarios, seeking the help of a family lawyer is helpful for better understanding and managing these issues.

Job loss: Gambling addiction can lead to unemployment. Staying absent during regular working hours or gambling online at work can lead to termination of services. Always follow company policies and standard operating procedures.

To manage this legal issue, it is essential to contact a professional layer of legal advisors who can help you. It is vital for mitigating legal problems.

Social dishonor caused by gambling addiction

Gamblers often experience social dishonor because they are perceived as unable to contribute to society. This stigma can have a negative impact on their behavior. Facing this challenge requires intense struggles on both an individual and societal level.

Effects of society on individuals

In developed and educated societies, gamblers can benefit from support and resources to overcome addiction. In contrast, in underdeveloped communities, where gambling problems are not well understood, support may be limited. In certain communities, where gambling is strictly prohibited, strict laws are enforced to discourage the habit.

How to cope with social challenges?

- **Public awareness:** Public awareness campaigns are essential to educate the population about gambling addiction and treat it as a serious problem.
- **Support groups**: Social groups can provide platforms for people struggling with gambling addiction, where they can share experiences and suggestions.
- **Support from family and friends:** Sharing problems with loved ones can provide support and positive feedback.
- **Professional counseling:** Therapists who specialize in gambling can provide valuable support in the recovery process.
- **Support from religious leaders:** People with strong religious convictions may find spiritual support and guidance from their religious leaders.

The intersection of motivation and financial resources Combining cultural and artistic motivation and finances can lead to meaningful projects that enrich culture, promote diversity and stimulate community engagement. Responsible investment and philanthropy play a crucial role in this process, channelling funds into projects with social and environmental benefits. This intersection is a powerful example of the human potential to generate positive change, highlighting the importance of more conscientious capitalism and equitable social progress.

Gambling Addiction and the Risk of Suicidal Thoughts

One of the significant side effects of gambling addiction is suicidal thoughts due to serious mental health problems. Depression and anxiety trigger negative opinions of hopelessness resulting from financial loss and relationship destruction. When all these intense negative aspects accumulate, they often lead gamblers to believe that there is only one way left to end all these worries at once, by committing suicide.

Significant Reasons Leading to Suicide in Gambling Addiction

Below are the main reasons that lead to suicide and may become the last resort in certain situations for certain people.

Irrecoverable financial losses: Continuous financial losses over a long period of time can lead to hopelessness and eventually end in suicidal thoughts.

Shame and guilt: After losing all your wealth, health and family. Society and relatives consider them losers and try to avoid them. The player feels ashamed that he has become a loser and everyone laughs at him. After feeling intense shame and guilt, the thought of self-harm was finally triggered.

Loss of relationships: Some people are compassionate and cannot stand the breakdown of meaningful relationships, such as divorce and entrusting children to another partner. The loneliness of loved ones can tear even an ordinary person apart.

Mental health disorder: Intense stress and depression, if left untreated, can trigger negative thoughts of suicide.

The importance of early realization and intervention

If gambling addiction is identified in the early stages, then it will be easy to recover. Early detection of problems has the points below.

Escalation Overview: Early detection of gambling addiction could be constructive not only to stop form escalation, but also to prevent the build-up of negative consequences.

Mental Health: Mental health problems, such as depression, could be avoided if gambling addiction is identified in its early stages. Co-current mental problems will also be prevented.

Support system: The support system will be planned and formulated accordingly once problems related to gambling addiction are addressed in advance.

Financial management: Early detection can also help gamblers be prepared to promptly manage debts before they accumulate and become unmanageable.

Eliminating the risk of suicide: Gamblers can prevent suicidal thoughts by addressing this risk early, before it becomes late.

Avoiding suicidal thoughts

Those affected (Gamblers), their families and friends need to be well aware of the problems related to gambling addiction and how they can cope with these problems.

There must be awareness campaigns in societies/communities to educate them in this regard. Thus, those players who are struggling to recover can be helped promptly.

With the help of family, friends, support groups, proper debt management, meditation, therapies, and ongoing efforts, they can quit their gambling addiction.

Quit gambling before it's too late. We only have one life; Give your life a second chance.

"The only solution to a gambling problem is to quit. Abandons. Close your hand. Break your habit, or it will break you." Hunter S. Thompson

The role of economics and morality in our lives

Life is like a complicated journey. It can be complicated, like a journey with many twists and turns.

Moral values can have economic reasons: Sometimes doing the right thing can be related to making money.

Governments invest in adult education for two reasons: When governments spend money educating adults, they don't do it just because they want to be excellent. It is also because having a well-educated population helps the country's financial situation. So it is a smart move that benefits everyone - it is a good thing and an excellent economic decision.

Acts of kindness have different motivations: When people do nice things, we feel good when we think they're just kind-hearted. But it's worth considering other reasons why they might do so. Sometimes people help others because it makes them feel emotionally healthy or connects with their spiritual beliefs. Realizing this does not mean that we are negative; It only helps us understand the world better.

Gambling is more about making money than helping the gambler: In the world of overcoming gambling addiction, the good-looking and exciting parts of gambling are primarily about making money, not really helping the person gambling.

Balanced vision helps recovery and growth: Seeing things in a balanced way is super helpful when you're trying to heal from something like gambling addiction. It reminds you to make choices based on your values and long-term well-being, instead of being fooled by how things might look or what seems morally right. It helps you make smarter choices for yourself.

Player life is not simple

A player's life is no ordinary one; This suggests that we should not treat it as usual, but as an extraordinary challenge. Every day starts for gamblers with the same continuous challenge. Indeed, something needs to change. There are people fighting within themselves who could, in fact, transform their lives. They are on the other side of the coin. Now they know freedom and success; They can shape their day and life according to their will. This is the most authentic way to live, as opposed to the misery and sadness of the gambling addiction cycle.

Life is fleeting; If we're in our forties now, we only have 10-15 productive years left before we end our journey. Therefore, if we really want change, the right time to act is now, not later, when we might lack both energy and time. Therefore, we should ask ourselves the question: when should we turn to the other side of the coin, building a new life without gambling? We only have one life, so why waste it and not make it useful? Let us think not only of ourselves, but also of children, wives, parents, friends, relatives, society, country and even globally. We can make a difference. It depends on our efforts.

Mostly "Never" or "Rarely": Your gaming habits might not worry you, but it's always wise to stay alert and in control.

A mix of 'Sometimes' and 'Never': You may show the first signs of problem gambling. It's a good idea to reevaluate your habits and perhaps seek guidance.

Mostly 'Often' or 'Regularly': Your responses suggest the possibility of compulsive gambling. Seeking professional support and connecting with a gambling addiction specialist could be beneficial for you.

Reflection on Gaming Habits: A Guide to Reflection

We've compiled this gentle but thorough self-assessment to help you take a close look at your gaming habits. By answering these questions honestly, you will gain valuable information about your relationship. with gambling. Remember, this is a safe space for reflection.

1. Frequency and duration: How often do you catch yourself gambling and how long do these sessions usually last?

o Less frequently and in the short term.

o Regularly and for increasingly longer periods of time.

o Very often and for long periods.

2. Financial management: Do you notice spending more money on gambling than you planned or can you comfortably afford it?

o Rarely.

o Occasionally.

o Quite often.

3. Loss tracking: After losing money, do you feel compelled to play again to regain it?

o Not really.

o Sometimes.

o Frequently.

4. Impact on responsibilities: Your activities Have gambling interfered with your professional or personal life, such as missing essential events?

o Not at all.

o From time to time.

Oh yes, it happened quite often.

5. Money loan: Have you had to borrow money, sell things, or put into savings intended for other purposes to support your gambling?

o Never.

o A few times.

o More times than I would like to admit.

6. Lying about gambling: You are in a position to keep your activities secret. gambling towards close ones?

o Never.

o From time to time.

o Quite often, actually.

7. Escape mechanism: Do you turn to gambling to escape stress, anxiety or problems in your life?

o Rarely.

o Sometimes.

o It's a frequent escape for me.

8. Inability to stop: Have you tried to stop or control your gambling, but found it hard to stick to it?

o I haven't tried.

o I tried and succeeded.

o I tried, but it was hard.

9. Mood Changes: Your Activities Gambling leads to noticeable changes in your mood.

o Almost never.

o From time to time.

o Yes, quite significant.

10. Impact on relationships: Has gambling created problems or conflicts in your relationships?

o Not really.

o There were some problems.

o It caused significant problems.

11. Financial consequences: Have you faced serious financial difficulties, such as debt or bankruptcy, due to gambling?

o Never.

o Once or twice.

o It happened repeatedly.

12. Withdrawal symptoms: When you don't gamble, do you have symptoms such as irritability or restlessness?

o Not at all.

o Occasionally.

o Quite regularly.

13. Neglect of other activities: Have you found yourself neglecting hobbies or self-care because of gambling?

o No.

o Sometimes.

o It happens often.

14. Feelings of guilt or remorse: Do you often feel guilty or remorse after playing?

o Rarely.

o Sometimes.

o Quite frequently.

15. Taking risks in gambling: Have you taken more considerable risks or made bigger bets over time?

o Never.

o From time to time.

o It has become commonplace.

Reflect on your answers:

Remember, this self-assessment is a starting point for self-reflection, not a clinical diagnosis. Recognizing any troubling patterns in your behavior Gambling is a brave first step. Seeking professional help can be helpful for recovery and regaining control of your life.

The dangers of gambling ads: A call for awareness

In the glamorous world of gambling, advertisements play a subtle but powerful role. The gambling industry, driven by its massive economic interests, uses marketing strategically to attract more people into the risky and often misleading world of gambling.

It's hard not to notice these ads, which are ubiquitous, from TV spots to online banners, creating a network of temptations that are difficult to avoid. These ads portray gambling as an exciting and easy path to prosperity, skillfully masking the grim realities of addiction and financial loss.

One of the main concerns is the impact of these advertisements on young people. Pervasive, they capture the attention of children and adolescents, potentially arousing an interest in gambling, which can culminate in addiction. The more ads are present, the greater the risk of seducing a younger audience towards gambling.

The industry isn't limited to advertising tactics. Placing advertisements and gaming venues in crowded areas and popular environments maximizes exposure, attracting numerous people who otherwise wouldn't have thought about gambling.

The victims of this advertising trap are often judged harshly. Society tends to blame them for their addiction, seeing it as a personal deficiency. But in reality, many are victims of a deliberate strategy on the part of an industry that profits from their involvement, regardless of the personal cost.

Recognizing the profound impact of advertisements is crucial in addressing gambling addiction. Being aware of the tactics used can help identify the external pressures fueling addiction, changing our perspective on how we view and treat gambling, and providing support and empathy to those affected.

In the context of the ubiquity of gambling advertisements, parents have a key role to play in protecting children from these influences. The increasing accessibility and commercialization of gambling presents parents with the challenge of shielding their children from their deceptive charm.

Controlling media exposure is a vital first step, involving limiting access to certain websites and TV channels. Using parental controls can help by filtering gambling-related content.
But limiting access is not enough. It is essential for parents to talk openly with their children about the realities of gambling, debunking myths and exposing risks. This education is crucial to demonstrate that gambling is neither a sure path to wealth nor a harmless pastime, but a risky activity with serious consequences.

Open and honest communication is key. Parents should explain how gambling ads are designed to attract and deceive, emphasizing the importance of critical thinking about these messages.
Promoting healthy entertainment alternatives and ways to reduce stress can steer children away from gambling, providing positive experiences that counteract the appeal of gambling.

Creating an environment of trust and support is also fundamental, encouraging children to discuss any gambling-related content they encounter, providing guidance and support instead of criticism.
Parents play a crucial role in protecting children from gambling advertisements. By managing access to media, educating, encouraging open communication and promoting positive activities, parents can effectively protect their children from gambling illusions and avoid potential harm.

Summary

Gambling addiction is a complex and profound challenge that requires a multidimensional approach to provide effective support to those affected. This expanded summary explores the main topics and ideas presented in the context of gambling addiction, providing insights and solutions for people struggling with this condition.

The Nature and Impact of Gambling Addiction

Gambling addiction is described as an intense and difficult struggle that requires willpower, determination and sustained efforts to overcome. The problem becomes even worse for those individuals who, for various reasons, including emotional exhaustion or lack of resources, find themselves unable to get out of this vicious circle.

Societal and Cultural Challenges

The situation is complicated in societies where there is cultural prejudice against gamblers, where they are stigmatised and treated as criminals rather than individuals in need of assistance and care. This stigma adds an extra layer of difficulty to the recovery process, isolating those affected and preventing access to necessary help.

The role of Education and Information

The proposed book addresses this issue directly, providing a valuable resource for people struggling with gambling addiction, but also for those around them who want to provide support. By explaining in detail the nature of addiction, how it can be identified, treated and managed, the book positions itself as a comprehensive guide to understanding and addressing this condition.

Treatment approach

Emphasizing the importance of home treatment and personalized approaches, the book recognizes that recovery is a unique process for each individual. By providing answers to essential questions – what, when, how, where and why gambling addiction should be treated – the author lays the foundation for an accessible and effective recovery strategy that can be tailored to each person's specific needs.

Inspiration si Motivation

The book also incorporates a motivational dimension, exemplified by Jeff Bezos' decision to leave the security of a stable job to pursue his entrepreneurial dream. This example highlights the value of taking calculated risks and overcoming fear of failure, principles that can be applied in the recovery process from gambling addiction.

Conclusion

The abstract highlights the need for an empathetic and well-informed approach to help people affected by gambling addiction. By promoting education, understanding and personalized support, the book aspires to become an essential tool for those seeking to overcome addiction and rebuild a balanced and fulfilling life. In the process, Bezos' story serves as a powerful reminder that regardless of obstacles, trial and perseverance can pave the way to success and personal fulfillment.

Part 3: From Player to Successful Entrepreneur

Becoming a successful businessman involves a series of strategic steps and deep dedication. This requires creating well-defined strategies, arranging the necessary resources, developing quality products or services, building a personal branding strategy, and managing market saturation in a way that brings satisfaction and success. The advantages of starting your own business are multiple, offering not only a way to get away from harmful activities such as gambling, but also to keep on the road to success.

To become a successful entrepreneur, it is essential to start with a solid plan, secure the necessary financing, fulfill all legal formalities, produce and market high-quality products or services, and be prepared to adjust plans according to market developments. It is crucial to assess risks and focus on risk and return analysis, monitor competition, cultivate creativity and remain consistent throughout the entrepreneurial journey.

Taking on a leadership role in your own business means becoming your own boss and having a team working under your guidance. To achieve success, it's vital to become an expert in your field, prioritize customer focus, and love what you do. Learning from competitors' experiences, motivating your team, and managing stress are also key components of business success.

As you develop as an expert in your field, the stress associated with business begins to ease. Becoming an expert quickly can greatly reduce difficulty times. Business planning must include creating a product or service with high demand in the market, ensuring its high quality and effective promotion.

To be a successful businessperson, it is essential to have quality products or services, an adequate target market, capital and a dedicated team, as well as a solid network of customers and suppliers. Networking can play a crucial role in business expansion. It is possible to start a business with limited resources, exemplified by starting an online freelancing business in the field of tutoring.

While it's not possible to compete directly with successful tycoons like Bill Gates, Steve Jobs, Mark Zuckerberg and Elon Musk, the key is to start with the resources available. Mark Zuckerberg, for example, started with a modest investment to become one of the richest businessmen in the world. This story emphasizes the importance of starting small and gradually building towards success.

How to become a successful entrepreneur

Starting a journey into the world of entrepreneurship, although it may seem intimidating at first, opens the door to significant rewards, such as autonomy in pursuing personal aspirations and the ability to make strategic choices towards success. This journey requires the clear expression of motivations and talents, inviting entrepreneurs to discover and align their passions and competencies with business goals. By combining skills and passions, unique profiles can be created that make a valuable contribution to the success of the business.

Developing a robust business plan is essential, requiring tailoring sections to specific objectives, thoroughly documenting and setting realistic goals. Identifying market needs, defining target audiences and implementing effective marketing strategies are crucial steps in this process.

Access to adequate resources, including financing, partnerships and expert advice, is the foundation for launching a business. Collaborating with professionals and identifying the right resources provides a solid foundation for success.

Building a personal brand strategy involves creating an attractive and authentic brand that communicates the values, mission and differentiators of the business. Maintaining consistency in visual style and tone of communication is vital to building a strong brand image.

Finally, continuous learning skills and adaptation to changes in the industry are essential to stay relevant in a dynamic business environment. This includes developing flexibility, innovation, adaptability and teamwork, ensuring entrepreneurs can effectively navigate emerging challenges and opportunities.

In conclusion, becoming a successful businessman requires a combination of self-discovery, strategic planning, access to appropriate resources, development of a strong personal brand

and a constant dedication to learning and adaptation. These elements, when approached with an open perspective and a willingness to learn from each experience, can pave the way for significant achievements in entrepreneurship.

Exploring passions and skills to become a businessman

Start by thinking about what you are good at and what you like to do; Your skills and passions can be an excellent basis for your business idea. Think about those activities that bring you fulfillment and joy. Explore your deep interests and passions; That inner fire motivates you and makes you feel in your element. This can indicate the direction you should find in your career. business.

Quoting Walt Disney, "All our dreams can come true if we dare to pursue them."

This remarkable quote emphasizes that courage and determination can make someone's dream come true. Identifying your passions It will guide you to an area where you can work warmly and you will be willing to invest your efforts and time to set up your business.

In addition to passions, it is imperative that you also know your abilities. Reflect on your previous job and personal experiences that helped you develop certain skills. These may include technical skills, such as programming, graphic design, or marketing, or interpersonal skills, such as effective communication, negotiation, and leadership. Exploring interests outside of business can provide a more grounded perspective.

Albert Einstein inspires us with the words: "Do not strive to be successful, but rather a man of value."

This reminds us that our values, skills and passions can make a significant contribution to business. Find a company that allows you to productively use your talents and bring value into the lives of others. To find the right business direction, consider the following questions:

What are your permanent desires?

Who will your target customers be and what problems does your business solve?

What skills and passions will be needed?

In which areas do you have strong expertise and experience?

And where do you feel confident in what you can achieve?

Who is your competitor in the market?

How can you collaborate with your passion and skills to bring about valuable change in that field?

How will you generate income and what is the source of funding?

What type of business appeals to you?

Is there an area that aligns with your passions where you can creatively use your ideas and skills?

Feel free to imagine, and being open brings new ideas. Choose a direction that allows you to advance, develop and share your unique perspective on the business world. Next, we will find a way to combine skills and passions to create a developed business. A simple method to check passion is to think about whether there are no money or time constraints for what you want to do. So the first answer that comes to mind is your passion, which makes you happy. In daily activities, think about what moment or act you like the most; It could be your passion.

Now, link to the skill you're an expert at or the task you can easily perform. Let's take a simple example: a travel vlogger. She loves to travel, so why not learn video editing and graphic design to post travel blog videos on social media?

With such a simple step, he could become a vlogger who not only enjoys traveling to various places, which is his passion, but also learns video editing, which he posts on YouTube and Facebook to earn money online. For a businessman, success could be his passion. Therefore, passion is the most essential driving force to achieve your goals.

The steps below will help you understand this process.

1. **Self-analysis to identify interests and passions:**

First, start by taking time for self-reflection. Reflect on what makes you happy; Think about your interests, hobbies, and what you like. Now, remember those flashes when you felt a genuine sense of accomplishment. Think about it: what was that event?

Recall your memories and try to find somewhere where your passion/desire was together at a particular moment.

2. **Assisting skills:**

Make a list of what you are currently good at doing, and mention complex skills (e.g. technical expertise - programming) and soft skills (e.g. communication skills, leadership skills).

Ask for advice and suggestions from friends, family mentors or colleagues. Occasionally, they see talents in us that we don't see in ourselves.

Find out where you can improve. Recognize parts that may need improvement.

3. **Discover areas where you can put your skills and passions to the test at work:**

Explore various business areas and niches to identify the most appropriate direction that meets your interests and passions. Think carefully about the impact you want to have in the industry and the ethical principles you want to follow in your work. Professional.

4. **Correlating your passions with your skills:**

Discover the area of work where you can apply your skills in pursuit of passion and success. Reflect on how your skills work. They can handle challenges.

5. **Instructions from leaders/experts:**

Meet with some top leaders in your field. Talk to them about how they did it, what challenges they faced, and how they overcame them.

Grab those ideal knowledge tips that can light your way for your trip.

6. **Portray your accomplishments in your mind:**

Be prepared to meditate. Visualize your dream business trip with your eyes open. See yourself facing contests; Fighting these challenges ultimately leads to success.

Practice this concept therapy, seeing it as a tool to explain your goals and promises for this exciting revolutionary path.

7. **Learn and share knowledge:**

Always share your teaching and ideas with others. Don't keep your thoughts to yourself, but discuss them with trusted associates, advisors, or advisors.

And let them share their ideas to refine your thoughts on how your imagination ties in. of real-life matters.

Always remain open, like those lights that could be helpful to others.

8. **Embrace the learning journey:**

Always try to learn new things. Try to educate yourself continuously. Be aware of industry trends, learn new skills, and always stay hungry for awareness.

You can participate in workshops, development courses or consultations. It's like an addition to your skill set; Adopt this growth mindset and be adaptable and flexible.

9. **Contact networks:**

Networking is essential in any aspect of the business world, whether you are looking for a job, opening a new business or pursuing success and personal development. Connect with professionals in your field. by participating in networking events, webinars and interactions with people who share your interests. or offer a different set of skills. Networking is not limited to exchanging business cards; It's about building relationships that can facilitate team collaboration, mentorship, and potential business partnerships.

10. **Action time:**

When you've gained a clear picture of your wants, skills, and those thrilling business concepts, it's time to take the leap. Start small and gradually increase the pace once you achieve some success with your plan. Keep a sense of initiative and be prepared to adjust your progress based on feedback and evolving market senses. You can showcase your passions and skills through these phases, laying the foundation for a determined, rewarding and exciting journey towards thriving entrepreneurship.

The next vigorous step in becoming an entrepreneur is to generate a solid plan for the industry. A well-crafted business plan will be your strategic guide, giving you clear direction and steps to get up and running your business.

In Zig Ziglar's world, "A goal without a plan is just a dream."

The business plan helps you turn your dream into a clear and achievable goal. It is essential to organize your ideas, identify the strengths and weaknesses of your business. and give you more effective strategies to achieve your goals and objectives.

In making your business plan, here are some key aspects you should follow:

Set your goals: Describing clear and precise goals is the first step in creating a business plan. First, it would be helpful to think about what you want to accomplish with your business. and set specific, measurable, achievable, relevant and time-bound (SMART) goals.

Market Review: Conduct a market examination to understand customer needs and preferences, industry trends, and companions. Know the market segments of your target audience and evaluate opportunities and fears.

Define the value scheme: Clearly and specifically define the unique values you offer. What kind of services or products do you offer to customers and how do you differentiate yourself from competitors? Make sure you understand your customer's needs and expectations. and that you are committed to providing the highest quality solutions.

Marketing and sales plans: Implement effective marketing and sales strategies and tactics to promote your business and attract customers. It's essential to select the right marketing channels, define clear key messages, and identify ways to engage your target audience.

Business and operations structure: Examine the design of your business and know the resources and capabilities needed to implement your plan. Pay attention to the financial resources, equipment, suppliers, and personnel needed to operate your business effectively.

Financial plan: Create a valuable financial plan that includes the source of revenue of the funds, cash flow statements, expense projections, initial investment estimates and profitability. Be realistic about your goal and ensure a sound financial strategy.

Monitoring and evaluation: Develop systems and metrics to examine and evaluate the performance of your business. Set aside some time to track progress and adjust your business plan based on results.

Henry Ford encourages us: "There is no secret to success. This is the result of preparation, hard work and learning from failure."

This quote reminds us that good planning and reliable execution are essential to building a successful business.

Creating a well-thought-out and detailed business plan will serve as a guiding guide on the road to a successful business. Make sure you cover all aspects and tailor your program to your specific business needs and goals.

Essential resources to start your journey in business

Exploring the necessary resources is vital to your transformation into a successful business. Fundamental factors such as land, labor, capital, and entrepreneurship are essential resources to starting a business. By trusting the discovery of these resources, you can increase your chances of achieving optimistic results in your industry.
Here are some steps and tricks for identifying and using resources:

Funding resources: Financing is an essential aspect of starting a business. Explore available funding sources, such as personal savings, bank loans, outside investors, or government financing programs. Develop a robust financial plan that includes cost and revenue estimates, as well as ways to access necessary financing resources. Initially, it would be prudent to have access to long-term finance; Afterwards, you can explore short- and medium-term financing options. Long-term financing involves taking out loans from financial institutions, which represent debt. It is necessary to regularly pay interest on borrowed funds. You can also obtain funds from internal sources, from partners or by listing the company's shares on the stock market. The general public may purchase these shares, which may be common or preferential. Shareholders will periodically receive dividends as a return on their investment. In case of losses, they will be distributed equally among shareholders.

> "Financial resources are not the problem, but the solution. They are the tool that helps you realize your dreams and build your business."
> -Robert Kiyosaki.

Team building: You must have strong team-building skills and be well prepared for a successful business. Explore staffing needs and look for the right people to share your vision and contribute their skills and experience. Select individuals with complementary talent, passions and skill sets. Be open to working with specialists and be well trained in different areas to support your business. Human resource management helps collect, select and develop talent. Therefore, the HR manager must find the right person for the right job.

Steve Jobs said, "Don't build your business on talented people; Find talented people to build your business."

Suppliers and partnerships: Explore the best suppliers and business partners who can provide you with the necessary sources and services. Always find a reliable partner and establish a solid relationship based on trust and mutual benefits. Provide value in your relationship. with suppliers and business partners to build a sustainable and successful collaboration. You need to select your suppliers carefully, because the quality of raw materials will be reflected in the final product and will eventually end up in the hands of your customers. If they are not satisfied with the quality, you will lose sales. Eventually, losses will be incurred. On the other hand, if you find cheap and suitable raw materials, the cost of production will decrease, and the price of the product will be lower than that of competitors, which will ultimately lead to customer satisfaction. Richard Branson said, "You can't do everything alone. It's important to find loyal partners to support you in your business."

Experienced advisors: Always establish strong relationships with well-specialized mentors to benefit from their expert advice and experience. They can provide you with business strategies, marketing, human resources, financing and legal guidance. Always seek technical advisors with domain knowledge and use their insights to improve your business and avoid common industry mistakes. Advisors are key staff members who can make or break your business empire. Your CEO/Head of Business/Manager could help you make rational business decisions taking into account current market trends, whether it's launching a new product or stopping manufacturing underperforming products. A marketing manager could help you advertise your products/services to a maximum number of potential customers. He will promote your products so everyone knows what you offer so they can buy. Usually, different organizations make their marketing budget taking into account the nature and dynamics of their business.

HR managers need to find the best staff for their business. They produce a SOP workbook "standard operating procedures" for work in discipline, control and organization. Financial managers/advisors help you find low-cost funds to borrow and high-yield investments to invest. They also record all expenses and income for a certain period and conduct periodic financial analysis from the financial statements prepared by accountants. These financial statements, such as the balance sheet, show the financial position of the company and the financial results of the company over a certain period.

Legal advisors handle the company's legal and statutory matters, including making arrangements and finalizing legal paperwork. Be determined and dedicated to seeking the resources needed for your business. Be open to opportunities and collaborate with highly specialized experts who can help your business grow and succeed. by sharing their experience and knowledge. Always remember that resources are not just tools; They can also be potential partners and supporters on your journey. business.

Develop a personal brand and marketing strategy

It is a vital aspect of your journey to a successful business. Explore a strong, defining personal brand that reflects your core business values and motto. Creating a great marketing strategy to help you attract and retain loyal and reputable customers is also very important. Marketing is useful for business. No one knows that you offer such services when you make a product or think about offering a service. Very few people can know about it. So, markup services are necessary to promote your product/services in the market. Different techniques are used to promote products, such as leaflet distribution, billboards, wall controls and promotion on radio, cables and televisions. You can advertise your products. on social networks such as Facebook, Instagram and YouTube.

Here are some steps on how you can accomplish these essentials.

Explore your personal brand identity: Establish the value of your business. Think about the goals that set you apart and the values you promote. Build an authentic and fascinating narrative that highlights your brand identity and personality.

Jeff Bezos said, "Your most valuable brand is what people say about you when you're not in the room."

Create a logo and visual identity: Invest in high-end design for your brand logo and optics. Make sure they can positively influence your brand's promotion. by using the best colors, typography, and elements that align with your brand's promotion. and reflects customers.

Verbal communication and marketing strategy: Deliver your message in such a way that it appeals to your customers and audience. Find the best communication channels for promoting your business and brand. and create relevant and engaging content. Use social media, likes forms, blogs, email marketing, or influencer collaboration to promote your business and brand and build a supportive community.

Richard Branson said, "You don't sell the products, you sell the story behind them."

Build solid relationships with your customers: Focus on a strong and healthy relationship, pay attention to their needs and wants, and provide the best experience. Be active on social media to respond to their feedback and questions. Develop a strong group around your brand. promoting loyalty and positive recommendations.

Monitor and adjust your marketing strategy: Always examine the performance of your marketing strategy and make adjustments along the way to achieve success and the best outcome. Investigate critical parameters such as conversation rates, social media engagement, or customer feedback or questions, and use the information to boost your strategy.

Peter Drucker said, "Don't try to be better than the competition; Try to be different."

Building a solid personal brand and developing a reliable and effective marketing strategy will help you distinguish and attract customers accurately and persuasively. Invest time and resources in these areas, which will be vital to the success of your business.

Learning and gradually adapting as a businessman

As a businessperson, it is imperative that you continually learn in pursuit of knowledge and adapt to changes in the industry according to customer needs and mindsets. Continuous learning is the key to success in an active and modest business environment. The adaptive approach is typically used when businesses face difficulties in normal routine operations and the nature of the business becomes unpredictable due to customer needs, technological change, or political issues. So in these scenarios, the adaptive approach to business works. It is necessary to be in contact with customers to meet their needs. Customer feedback can serve this purpose. Contingency planning, insurance and diversification can be carried out taking into account the dynamic market environment if adaptation is needed.

Here are some useful things to follow:

Be open to learning: Always learning and developing skills; knowledge is more valuable than resources, which helps you make better-informed decisions and adapt to changing market demands. Always find training and personal development events such as courses, seminars, conferences or books that can help you expand your knowledge and improve your business skills.

> Albert Einstein said: "Learn from yesterday, live for today, hope for tomorrow. The most important thing is to never stop asking questions."

Examine trends and changes in the industry: Stay on top of trends and developments in your industry. Monitor its changes, new marketing techniques, and customer preferences, and adapt your plans accordingly.

Keep innovative technologies and their solutions in mind: Always find new and advanced technologies and find the best way to solve problems that increase the progress of your business. From manual processes to online and digital platforms and sales, new advancements can bring benefits for improving and managing your business.

Be innovative and adaptable: You must be able to adapt or change according to changes in the market. Be open to facing customer feedback and questions and change according to their needs and changing market demands. The ability to change across industries and learn from experiences is critical to the growth and success of your business.

Charles Darwin said, "It is not the strongest or the smartest who are still surviving, but those who can best manage change."

Continuous learning is the key to success, keeping our business in step with market developments and ensuring long-term success. You have a better chance of realizing your business dream if you are open to new ideas, if you learn from another successful businessman and if you are constantly looking for adaptation and improvement.

Leverage in your current career

In this section, we'll discover that business leverage often refers to using different resources, such as capital, technology, or partnerships, to amplify the impact of your efforts. You will better understand that you can find satisfactory fulfillment in your current career without stakes. A successful leverage mobilization requires careful balance to minimize risk levels and at the same time increase return.

Business leverage is a combination of two words: business, the act of being busy or buying and selling for profit, and leverage, the concept in which, on the one hand, you make a small effort, and on the other, a significant result is observed. Thus, leverage helps you do more or achieve more results with less effort. Not everyone can be successful in business just by entering the market and starting a new initiative. It is essential to first identify what skills you possess at the highest level. Once you've recognized your strength, you can use this skill as a competitive advantage, capitalizing on it to ensure your success and growth in the marketplace.

The leverage can be qualitative, such as skills, or quantitative, for example, financial. In financial terms, suppose a local show producer bought a $2 million factory through collective investments of $200,000 and $1,800,000 monthly. He uses the financial leverage of the amount borrowed and does his business, although his company is risky because his investment is composed of less equity and more debt financing. He still generates a profit of 300K annually.

Always be aggressive in developing leverage. It could be automating your work, learning skills you're already an expert in, or turning you into a specialist in your field. Learning and adopting best practices in your industry It will be leveraged for you.

Here are some steps to use your leverage in your current career:

Setting professional goals: Specialized goals are the exact goals you aim to achieve in your profession. It would be helpful if you deliberated on what you want to understand and what path you want to take in your future career. These goals can range from getting new services and can inspire you to make an exact location or contribute to your business. in an expressive technique. Make your goal Being specific, relevant and time-limited is useful for effective planning and progress tracking.

Developing skills for better business performance: Skill development is a constant method containing intentional learning and practice to improve your capabilities. Try to invest in developing your skills and making changes to your professional performance. Attend online courses, specialized courses, seminars or training programs to develop your skills and advance your career.

Building a professional network in business: Creating and maintaining a professional network involves attending industry events, joining relevant online forums, getting professional associations and groups and platforms like LinkedIn, as well as being open to sharing experiences and expertise and learning from other professionals. Be proactive in promoting meaningful connections.

Taking on new responsibilities is a lifelong learning process: Look for opportunities to take on new responsibilities and get involved in exciting projects within your current business. Approach challenges with a positive mindset and adaptability to ensure success. This will give you a unique chance and track to develop and demonstrate your skills and potential.

Finding job satisfaction: Always remember that job satisfaction is a dynamic process, and it's important to periodically reevaluate and adjust as needed. Find and explore new ways to achieve happiness at your current job. If you follow a few regular steps, you can achieve a high level of satisfaction, namely, set clear goals, develop skills, build relationships, maintain a work-life balance, seek challenges, communicate with your superiors, take breaks.

Whether you want to become an entrepreneur or influence your profession, in order to realize yourself as a business specialist, you emphasize creating a lasting connection, permanent knowledge of the market and trends, and constantly increasing skills. Expose yourself to new opportunities and acquire your skills and other involvements. Continue to refine your business acumen and consider mentoring or professional development programs to boost your strategic thinking and decision-making skills. This chapter will guide you through this process.

The concepts mentioned above are explained in detail below.

Defining professional goals

Defining goals is the first step to the success of your business, but setting your professional goal is more critical. At this stage, reflecting on your passions, values and aspirations is more important than setting transparent and authentic goals to guide your career.

You need to have some main goals in your career, which can be short, medium and long term. The SMART methodology is also considered the best for this purpose. Your goals They must be specific and have some solid details, be measurable, achievable and relevant to your vision. You also need to set deadlines to achieve these goals.

Here are some points to set your goals:

Reflect on your passions and values: Start by reflecting on what motivates and inspires you in your field. Think about your mottos. and the things you enjoy doing, as well as the values you consider very important in your career.

Set Smart Goals: Smart goals are more authentic, achievable, specific, and time-limited. This approach helps you formulate your plans in a real and easy-to-follow manner. Set a measurable standard to help you evaluate progress toward your goals.

Categorize your goals: List your goals in order, identifying the ones that are most important and will bring the most significant benefits to your professional progress. Focus your resources and efforts on these essential goals.

Develop an action plan: Find the right steps to achieve each goal and make a timeline for each stage of your action plan. Be flexible and adapt according to the needs of the plan.

Review and review: Review your progress and action plan regularly, adjusting your strategies and tricks as needed. Be open to feedback and improvement as you get closer to your goals.

T. Havre Iker said, "Your dreams are outside your comfort zone. You have to get out of your luxury zone to achieve your goals."

Clarifying your qualified goals is a vigorous stage in your journey to professional success. With a robust set of goals and a defined action plan, you'll be on the exact path to turning your thoughts into authenticity and realising your full potential in your career.

Skill improvement and progression

Improving and developing your skills, as well as increasing your professional performance, are crucial to your career success. Investing in personal and professional growth brings significant development, facilitating the achievement of professional goals. Here are some steps you can take to develop your skills and improve your performance.

Recognising skills gaps: Be honest with yourself and identify areas where you need improvement. These may include specific technical skills, leadership capabilities or other aspects relevant to your field of activity. Identifying these gaps will allow you to focus your efforts appropriately.

Participation in specialized training programs and courses: Be active in the search for learning and development opportunities by participating in specialized training programs, seminars or courses. Choose programs that focus on the skills and competencies you want to develop.

Learn from successful people and experiences: Always study and learn from the experience and knowledge of professionals in your field. Reading biographies, watching interviews, or attending events where these experts share their perspectives and advice can be valuable ways of learning and inspiration.

Warren Buffet said, "You can't be successful if you don't learn from the best."

Put into practice and apply the acquired knowledge: learning does not stop at a course or attending seminars. It is imperative that you apply your knowledge and practice your acquired skills. Find different opportunities within the Owen business or other professional projects to use your skills to improve your performance.

Be open to face-to-face feedback and self-knowledge: Face productive input and try to develop self-knowledge. Be proactive in receiving suggestions and take experience from colleagues, clients, or mentors. Regular self-assessment can help you examine your strengths and weaknesses and focus on ongoing development.

Increasing your skills and improving your professional performance helps you get back on your feet. Stay in constant search for learning and development opportunities and you will be able to reach your full potential in professional activities.

Building a professional network

A strong network is essential in a professional career. A well-known network of contacts can provide you with business opportunities, support and guidance. To connect you with people with valuable experience and knowledge, here are some steps to maintaining a solid professional network.

As a new entrepreneur, you should be interconnected with other entrepreneurs with industry experience to learn from them. A network of professionals from the same sector can contribute significantly to business success. As a new entrepreneur, you need to establish better relationships with other fellow entrepreneurs in the industry; They will surely guide you on how to use your resources in the best way to achieve your business goals.

Strong relationships with the network boost your career and open doors to new opportunities. You need to choose the network that suits you best; An operational, personal or strategic network is right for you. You need to adopt a "give and give" approach while connecting with networks. Always try to build relationships with other people in the industry, even strangers, bond with them and focus on mutual benefits.

Attend business events: Be energetic in the business community and attend relevant network events. These events allow you to meet and interact with other experts in business and your field. Be open to sharing your experience and learning from other experts.

Attach yourself to professional associations and groups: Find professional social media platforms like Linkedin to expand your business networks. And interact with other professional businessmen from various fields.

Porter Gale said, "Your network is your net worth."

Become a good listener and communicator: You should build an excellent image in business. You have solid communication skills. Be realistic and open in your interaction with others, listen carefully and show interest in the perspectives and experiences of others. Always show your willingness and happiness to offer support and help where possible.

Developing a solid network takes more time and effort. But ultimately, it can change your life and business in the industrial field. And you'll see how your network is running smoothly. expands and supports you on your journey. towards business success, taking on new responsibilities to grow your business.

Finding opportunities to take new steps and get involved in exciting projects within your current job is significant. This boldness will help you develop professionally and prove your skills and potential.

As a new entrepreneur, get support from your networks, research your area of interest and get some training. Keep up to date with new opportunities in the field. Improve your strengths and reduce your weaknesses. Communication plays a significant role in business success, while discussing issues with your team, meeting with partners or suppliers, or conducting promotional interviews each time you depend on good communication skills. Teamwork and good decision-making skills are also useful for business success.

Here are some tips for taking on new responsibilities and projects:

Be proactive and engaged: Don't wait for opportunities to arise. Take action, look for opportunities to get involved in new projects, and take on additional organizational responsibilities. Show your interest, passion for new challenges and willingness to actively participate.

Find organizational needs and gaps: Pay close attention to cracks and points where your requirement is needed. This could involve initiatives to improve existing processes, projects to solve identified problems, or margins to support the growth and development of the organization.

Reveal confidence and ability: When you take on new responsibilities or steps in the organization, you can be prepared to take calculated risks. Show that you are willing to learn and develop as you take care of tasks and reveal your commitment to the success of the project you are involved in.

Connect with colleagues and other departments: Getting involved in new projects can also attach you with different departments or teams, or with your colleagues. Be open to connecting with others and learning from other experts. Share your ideas and work as a team to achieve success.

Learn from your seniors and ask for feedback: As you engage in a new responsibility, show your positive attitude by learning from other experts. And ask for feedback from your colleagues and managers. This information will help you develop and improve your skills in future projects.

Theodore Roosevelt said, "Do what you can, with what you have, where you are."

Always remember that taking on new responsibilities and projects is a vital step in growing your business. Be brave, get actively involved and find new opportunities to prove to yourself that your skills are growing in your professional career.

As you develop your business skills and find more career options, it's imperative to find a level of satisfaction in your current job/activity.

You are satisfied if you get involved in any business or job and get a good reward. If you are an expert in your work and feel satisfied with your current role, you will be satisfied. The environment, co-workers, culture of the organization and the nature of work are the main factors that influence the level of satisfaction. If you carry out useful work in a healthy environment and if your lifestyle is balanced, you meet all the necessary criteria for job satisfaction.

Here are some essential steps to finding job satisfaction:

1. Define what inspires and interests you: Pay attention to activities and projects within your job. that bring you more joy and happiness. Explore what you're most passionate about. Then,

focus on these aspects. You can try to get more projects that align with your interests and passions.

2. Take responsibility and initiative: Be active in your work and responsibilities for better future results. Find opportunities to contribute and make a positive impact within your organization. Be energetic to face new challenges and projects that motivate you.

3. Work together and build a relationship: Healthy relationships with your team and colleagues are vital to job satisfaction. Try to establish strong relationships with your colleagues. to obtain standard results. Participate in team activities and collaborative projects that allow you to work with other experienced and motivated professionals.

4. Find challenges and opportunities for growth: Don't expect job satisfaction to come from the comfort of your routine alone. Always look for new challenges and growth events in your work. Expand your responsibilities, learn new skills and get involved in projects that give you professional growth.

5. Celebrating successes and Recognition: Don't forget to mark your successes and appreciate yourself, which you deserve. Whether you're achieving an outstanding result or achieving your goals, celebrate these moments to remind yourself how much you can accomplish in your current job.

Sam Walton said: "There is no big secret to success at work. It's the work itself – finding satisfaction in what you do.

Finding job satisfaction is meaningful for motivating you to give your best. Be open to new opportunities for growth and development, and the best results await you.

Risk and reward

You like to take risks and make plans to overcome those risks. And transfer from the big loser to the big winner.

First, let's think about gambling. It is often seen as a quick money-making game, a chance to make large sums of money with little effort. But the reality is that gambling is a game of chance; Occasionally you're lucky, but in the long run, the house always wins. Because gambling is designed in such a way that there are always favors for casinos and bookmakers, not for players.

But on the other hand, taking risks in business doesn't mean recklessly throwing yourself into dangerous situations. It means carefully evaluating your options, gathering as much information as possible, and making decisions based on the knowledge you gather from different resources. It implies that captivating a projected risk with disappointment in mind is an opportunity, but with the hope that success is achievable.

This is a very significant feature of the industry. Without taking risks, there is no chance to develop or grow the business. Any successful business starts with a person willing to take risks, try new ideas, and always be ready to face failure. But with risk comes some benefits, and the incentive can be amazing for those who thrive.

So how can you alternate from a player to a professionally successful person? The first step is to rotate your attention and change your thinking that gambling is a technique to make money quickly; Start thinking of modified ways to operate your time currency and energy in building an effective business. Instead of trusting luck. Start to load yourself, skills and knowledge.

Second, start educating yourself, read about business and risk management, and gain additional knowledge about the industry you're entering. Learn from experts who have succeeded and try to understand what they did well.

Third, start taking a calculated risk. This means creating a side business, keeping a stable job, or investing a small amount of money in a new idea to see if it works.

Finally, don't get discouraged if you don't achieve immediate success. Achievement in business and in life is often a procedure of passion and mistake. The critical point is to learn from your mistakes and keep trying repeatedly.

Business risk-taking is more critical to success and sustainable strategy than gambling. Gambling is based on luck; Business success is based on making the best and most prosperous decisions and managing risks. By changing your mindset and starting to take calculated risks, you transfer from a player to a successful business person.

Think about the amount of money you spend over time. This is an essential and sometimes revealing reflection; It can help you understand the critical financial impact of these activities.

If you are still gambling, it is time to consider your losses and financial gains. This can be an excruciating exercise, but necessary to clearly understand your financial situation. Using a notebook or valuable app to track these transactions can be helpful.

It is essential to understand the dark side of gambling. The odds are often against us. The chances of success may be slim, while the chances of losing are very high. Usually, casinos or online gambling operators have certain advantages, so most players are in unfavorable positions.

What could you do with that money if you hadn't spent it on gambling or invested it in a successful business for great results? That money could have been invested in other ways that provide short- and medium-term financial benefits. You could start saving or investing in a savings account or stocks. You could offset your obligations or spend on your education or the education of your children. These choices could significantly progress your long-term economic future.

Therefore, reflecting on the money spent on gambling can serve as a wake-up call to understand how it might affect you in the long run and explore alternative financial paths to improve your financial future. It is an essential step in the awareness and decision-making process to end these gambling addictions and channel your resources in more constructive and financial directions.

In the past, this term was used to describe the intense business mindset. It reflects the passion, risk-taking and determination of businesses to pursue their goals. This mindset may involve a willingness to take on meaningful challenges. Humans will no longer be mere robots executing orders, but will become creators, bringing to the forefront what makes them human: interpersonal passions and skills. This transformation is remarkable in the successful business world. We know that insanity is not a symptom of stupidity. Madness can be an essential ingredient in the world of successful business. This madness refers to the courage to take risks in business.

The ability to think outside conventional patterns and innovate in the business world can be a competitive advantage. This madness will play a significant role in the development of successful businesses in the future. Traditional boundaries will no longer constrain people and they will be free to experiment and find innovative ideas, even those currently considered crazy. Their bold visions and seemingly eccentric ideas can lead to the discovery of new opportunities and revolutionary solutions that can radically change the way the business world works. Passion is a powerful driving force. It allows you to emotionally enjoy what you do and maintain a strong motivation to achieve your goals.

Any popular business is satisfied with passion for what it prepares, and this helps them overcome difficulties and stay attentive on their way. Knowledge is a crucial part of success. Continuous learning is also essential in an ever-changing world. Successful businessmen know they can't stop in the rapidly evolving environment. They are always eager to acquire knowledge, increase their skills and discover new strategies and techniques to improve their business. Business relationships are another significant component on the path to business success. Building and maintaining a network of contacts can give you business opportunities and support your mentorship and resources. Interacting with other businessmen and industry experts can bring insights and create synergies that lead to significant progress in the business world. The future of work will enable us to work as people, bringing creativity, passion and business skills to the forefront.

Madness shouldn't be a problem; It can be the key to innovation and success. With the courage to take risks and the right skills, you can become a successful businessperson and contribute to essential changes in the business world, turning useful ideas into everyday reality. The business industry is changing rapidly with innovations, technologies, new ideas, research and techniques in the modern era. The future of work has developed as an essential point for corporations to stay one step ahead.

Taking a closer look at this scenario, we find that Unilever, an international customer merchandise giant, has adopted a precautionary tactic to prepare for the transformative journey into the future. Unilever, renowned for its various product varieties, is not only familiar with the transformation but also dynamically influential. The idealistic approach to the corporation includes implementing new technical improvements and developing a culture of modernization. This arranges the platform for a job. Unilever knows that the future of the workplace isn't just about considering technology, it's also about accepting and responding to changing industry demands.

The future of jobs is about how jobs, businesses and jobs change in response to technological, social, political and cultural change. For example, remote work, robots that help with daily activities, and self-employment, where everyone could become their own boss in the dynamic economy. It's about predicting the future and planning accordingly.

The future of work extends beyond advances in high-tech. While innovative tools are vital, the essence lies in creating an atmosphere that respects cooperation, creativity and elasticity. It is as if it almost breaks rigid structures, creating a workplace where workers can freely express their opinions and enjoy the environment.

The ongoing dynamics of the future of work

The future of work is an exciting nature with extraordinarily changing aspects. The mix of virtual and physical jurisdictions is reforming work culture, making remote work the standard for many companies. Key developments include an in-depth focus on worker comfort, an increased dependence on artificial intelligence and automation, and a demand for digital expertise.

Factors influencing the future of work

The following are the main factors profoundly influencing the future of work.

1. Technology and its impacts: The future of work is directly linked to cutting-edge technologies such as artificial intelligence and robotics, revealing new heights of modernization.

2. Worker comfort: Identify employees as a company's most valuable asset; Increasing importance is given to the care of psychological well-being, elastic work measures, resourcefulness and cultivating the wisdom to feel satisfied.

3. Digital services revolution: As businesses go through digital revolutions, there is an acute demand for digitally skilled workers.

4. Hybrid work approach: Old-style office practices give way to elastic and cross-cutting work patterns, allowing staff to choose their ways of working.

Achieving an approach to the future of work

A Future of Work Plan is a comprehensive plan that addresses technical incorporation, talent development and social change within the association and encompasses upskilling of staff, concerted digital job creation and development of constant learning beliefs.

Corporations like Unilever are not only persisting in change, they are aggressively driving it. Purpose extends beyond persistence; It's about thriving in an emerging business industry. The issues that determine the future of work provide a roadmap for corporations to direct the madness and develop as leaders in this modern field.

With a healthy plan for the future of work, businesses can turn challenges into opportunities for growth. This confirms a sustainable and prosperous journey into the future, where speed, modernisation and flexibility are converted into assets.

Appreciating the simple things in life

In the labyrinth of modern life, where every day brings with it a new race for success, material achievement and social validation, we often get lost in a tumult of aspirations and expectations. Contemporary society, with its frenetic pace and obsession with material progress, pushes us to always seek more, to reach new peaks and to accumulate riches. In this ceaseless search, the essentials of life—simple beauty, quiet moments, unexpected pleasures—are often lost in the daily turmoil. This phenomenon is not only a feature of our times, but has become a way of life, a culture in which individual worth and achievements are measured in material terms and external success.

As society advances technologically and economically, the paradox of an interconnected but at the same time isolated world is created. We are more connected than ever through digital means, but authentic relationships and deep human experiences are being replaced by ephemeral interactions and shiny surfaces. In this digital age, time spent on social media, following the lives of others and comparing ourselves to unrealistic ideals promoted, has become the norm. This filtered virtual reality distorts our perception of authentic life and what really matters.

In this relentless search for more, for better, for faster, we lose touch with nature and its slow but steady rhythms. We get so caught up in our daily routine that we forget to notice the beauty of a sunset, listen to the stillness of a morning or feel the breeze blowing through the leaves of the trees. These simple joys, which require no financial effort and are accessible to everyone, are often overlooked in favor of material goals and tangible achievements.

Also, in this frantic search, we lose connection with our inner self. Instead of being present in the present moment, connecting with our emotions and thoughts, we are often distracted by outside noise. This leads us to a lack of self-knowledge and a misunderstanding of our own needs and desires. We are so preoccupied with living up to society's

expectations that we forget to ask ourselves what really makes us happy.
Moreover, this loss of connection to simple and authentic things has a significant impact on our mental health. Constant stress, pressure to always be "on top" and fear of not living up to expectations can lead to anxiety, depression and other psychological disorders. We are so worried about the future and what we don't have that we forget to live in the present and appreciate what we have.
Reconnecting with the simple things of life can be a journey of self-discovery and redefining priorities. Learning to appreciate the small pleasures of life, to be grateful for what we have, to enjoy the company of loved ones and to find peace in nature are important steps towards a balanced and fulfilled life. It involves a shift in perspective, from always looking for more, to being content and at peace with who is.
In this process, it is essential to take time to stop and reflect. Disconnecting from technology and reconnecting with nature and our selves can be a source of regeneration and inspiration. Nature walks, meditation, practicing gratitude, and spending time in silence can help clear the mind and refocus on what's really important.
By rediscovering the beauty and value of simple things, we can change the way we live and experience life. This does not mean giving up progress or aspirations, but finding a balance between them and moments of peace and simplicity. Appreciating the beauty of a starry sky, the quality of a conversation with a friend, the taste of a homemade meal, or the tranquility of an unhurried morning are all ways we can reconnect with the essence of life.

Reconnecting with the simple things is not only a path to a more balanced life, but also a form of resistance against the pressures of a society oriented towards consumption and materialism. Choosing to value authentic moments, deep human relationships and the beauties of nature is an act of affirmation of our own humanity and a rejection of a life governed exclusively by external and material goals. Rediscovering and appreciating the simple things of life can help us live with more awareness and presence, enjoy every moment, and find true happiness in the things that really matter. This is the path to a fulfilling life, where each day is lived with intention and gratitude, and where simple joys are the source of true fulfillment.

In the modern world, we are surrounded by a constant stream of advertising and marketing messages that shape and influence how we perceive success and happiness. This ubiquity of advertising not only urges us to buy and consume, but also creates an idealized image of what it means to be happy and fulfilled. These messages can lead us to believe that our worth as individuals is related to the goods we possess or our social status.

Advertising, by its nature, aims to persuade and manipulate, using eye-catching images, memorable slogans and often appealing to strong emotions to create a connection between product and consumer. It is an art form, but also a science, that studies human behavior to encourage consumption. In the process, it can distort our understanding of what is really important in life, placing disproportionate emphasis on material purchases.

Digital marketing, in particular, has brought this influence into our daily lives, being ubiquitous on social media platforms, emails, websites and apps. It is almost impossible to surf the internet without being exposed to advertisements, intensifying pressure to follow society's standards of fashion, lifestyle and success.

The effect of advertising ubiquity is complex. On the one hand, it inspires and informs us, but on the other hand, it can create a constant need to have more and better, generating an endless cycle of ephemeral desires and satisfactions, often described as a "hamster wheel" in search of happiness through consumption.
Another major impact of advertising is how it influences our perceptions of our own worth and those around us, encouraging people to be valued not by their character, but

by the assets they own. This can lead to a culture of envy and competition, where success and personal worth are measured in material terms.

To counter this influence, it is essential to develop awareness and discernment, recognizing when we are being manipulated by advertising messages and asking ourselves if the desires induced are really aligned with our authentic values and aspirations. It is important to remember that happiness and fulfillment cannot be bought, but come from experiences, relationships, personal achievements, and appreciation of life's beauty and simple joys.
The need to disconnect from the pervasive influence of advertising and reconnect with authentic values becomes a crucial step in the search for a balanced and fulfilling life. By becoming aware of and reducing the impact of these messages on our decisions and values, we can discover a clearer path to real happiness and personal fulfillment.

Living authentically is about living in harmony with our true feelings, thoughts and values. It involves finding joy in small things, such as a good conversation with an old friend, a relaxing walk in nature, or even quiet time spent thinking about yourself. These simple but deeply satisfying moments connect us with the essence of our human reality and give us a sense of peace and clarity, inaccessible in material goods. In a world that encourages us to always look for something bigger, better, or more spectacular, there is amazing beauty in recognizing and appreciating the value of everyday experiences. It doesn't mean giving up aspirations or goals, but balancing those ambitions with appreciating the moments and experiences that bring us true happiness.

Let's take the example of a family meal. In an era dominated by fast food and hasty meals, the act of cooking and dining with family becomes a gesture of rebellion against the accelerated pace of modern life, not only about food, but also about sharing experiences, laughing and building precious memories.

Similarly, appreciating nature's beauty offers immense benefits. A simple walk in the park or watching a sunset can help disconnect from daily stress and recharge emotionally and mentally. These moments allow us to be present, to reconnect with our inner selves, and to remind ourselves of the beauty and simplicity of the world around us.
Cultivating hobbies and personal interests is a form of authentic experience. Whether it is painting, writing, gardening or any other activity that brings us joy, these passions give us a refuge from the hustle and bustle of everyday life and allow us to express our creativity and individuality. In a world often distracted by the superficial glow of materialism, it is essential to remind ourselves and value the importance of authentic and simple experiences. They enrich our existence and bring us a happiness and fulfillment that no material object can provide.
Nature offers us some of the most beautiful gifts: the warm rays of the sun, the cool breeze of a summer day, the beauty of a natural landscape or the tranquility of a forest. These experiences, free but of immense emotional and spiritual value, reconnect us with nature and remind us of the rhythms of life.

Moments spent with family and friends bring a deep sense of accomplishment. Conversations, shared laughter, or quiet walks with a loved one strengthen bonds and provide emotional support.
Hobbies and creative activities allow us to explore and express deeper aspects of our personality, providing a break from our daily routine and helping us understand and process emotions.

Simple pleasures, such as reading, listening to music or cooking, are joys that enrich everyday life without great cost, adding immense value to our lives.
By valuing and cultivating these authentic experiences, we reconnect with our true values and live a more conscious and fulfilling life.

To truly appreciate these gratuitous joys, it is important to cultivate an attitude of mindfulness and gratitude. By being present in the moment and appreciating what we have, we can find happiness and fulfillment in simple things. This appreciation helps us balance our lives and find peace and joy despite the challenges and bustle of modern life. The free joys of life are essential aspects that enrich our existence and bring us genuine happiness. By reconnecting with these simple pleasures, we can live a more fulfilling and harmonious life, appreciating the beauty and generosity of the world around us. These experiences remind us that the most valuable things in life are not always the ones we can buy, but are often the ones we experience and feel.

Slowing down doesn't just mean reducing the speed at which we perform daily activities, but also giving ourselves the time to be truly present in the moments we are living. It involves full awareness of our experiences, feelings, and thoughts. It is the process of stopping the mind's uninterrupted race to the past or future and anchoring yourself in the "now," appreciating the beauty, simplicity, and wonder of the present.

In practice, slowing down can take many forms. It can mean taking a break from technology and digital media that constantly bombard us with information and keep us in a state of hyperconnectivity. It can mean choosing to spend time in nature, where the pace of life is dictated by natural cycles, not schedules and deadlines. Here, we can learn from the rhythms of nature, which, although slow, are always in motion and evolution.

Slowing down also involves rediscovering simple pleasures, such as enjoying a meal without haste, practicing a hobby, or simply sitting and contemplating the world around you. In these moments, we are discovering that many of life's most precious and fulfilling experiences do not require speed or efficiency, but presence and awareness.

This slowdown allows us to reconnect with ourselves. In the stillness and space created by slowing down, we can listen to our thoughts and feelings, reflect on our experiences, and gain a deeper understanding of what truly brings us joy and fulfillment. This process of self-discovery is vital for personal development and for cultivating a sense of inner peace and satisfaction.

In addition to personal benefits, slowing down also has a positive impact on our relationships. When we take time to truly be present with our loved ones, we build deeper and more meaningful connections. Active listening, empathy and sharing experiences become more authentic and enriching. Slowing down and appreciating moments in our lives is essential to living consciously and fully. It helps us balance our lives, reconnect with our essence and enjoy the beauty and wonders that surround us. By adopting a slower and more intentional pace of life, we can discover a source of joy and tranquility that contrasts sharply with the hustle and bustle of everyday life.

Human relationships are the basis of our life experience. The bonds we form with others define us, shape us and give us a sense of belonging and purpose. In our relationships we find support, love, understanding and compassion - essential elements for a balanced and fulfilling life.

In our family we often find the first level of support and acceptance. From the moments spent together at meals, holidays, and family events, to everyday conversations and small routines, family life enriches our existence and gives us a sense of stability and continuity. In these interactions, we learn fundamental values such as unconditional love, sacrifice, and giving.

Friends, on the other hand, are often our personal choice and reflect our preferences and values. They are partners in life's adventure, giving us a different perspective, advice, joy and sometimes even challenges that help us grow. True friends are those who accept us as we are and stand by us in good times and in difficult times.

In the digital age, with all its advantages, there is a risk of replacing authentic relationships with superficial interactions online. Social media can create the illusion of connection, but it often doesn't provide the depth and satisfaction that face-to-face interactions bring. Therefore, it is crucial that we strive to preserve and cultivate our real relationships by giving them time and energy.

The value of relationships lies not only in the happy and easy moments, but also in the challenges and difficulties we face together. In these moments, the quality and strength of our relationships are tested and strengthened. Sharing hardships, misunderstandings, and losses helps us build resilience and mutual understanding. Relationships are a fundamental element of a fulfilling life, bringing us joy, giving us a sense of security, and helping us navigate the complexities of life. By cultivating authentic relationships and valuing time spent with loved ones, we enrich our human experience and find balance and meaning in our lives. Relationships teach us about empathy, about giving and receiving, and about the beauty of sharing life with others. In this ever-changing world, they remain our constants, our sources of strength and joy.

Nature in all its forms – from a simple local garden or park to dense forests and high mountains – gives us a sense of peace and belonging to something bigger than ourselves. There is something deeply healing about listening to the murmur of a river, feeling the breeze on your skin, contemplating the beauty of a natural landscape, or walking along a trail through the forest. These experiences allow us to quiet our minds, clarify our thoughts and charge ourselves spiritually. Moreover, nature gives us valuable lessons about life and our place in the world. The rhythms of nature – the change of seasons, the life cycle of plants and animals, the simplicity and beauty of natural phenomena – remind us of the cyclicity and interconnectedness of life. In nature, we observe how each element plays a vital role in the ecosystem and how diversity and harmony coexist.

For many, nature is also a space for activities that bring joy and satisfaction. Whether it's gardening, hiking, landscape photography or simply observing wildlife, these activities allow us to express our creativity, explore passions and develop a deeper appreciation for the beauties of the world. Nature plays a crucial role in our physical and mental health, reducing stress, anxiety and depression, improving well-being and increasing energy levels. It is a space where we can rebalance and regenerate, away from the pressures of modern life. Nature is not just a setting for our activities or a backdrop for everyday life; It is a vital refuge, a space of retrieval and reconnection. By appreciating and protecting the natural environment, we not only enrich our own lives, but also contribute to the well-being of future generations. The role of nature in our lives is indispensable and profoundly transformative, providing us with a place of refuge and peace, reminding us of the beauty and wonders of the world, and helping us find balance and harmony in an often chaotic and overburdened world.

Time, unlike other resources, is finite and irreversible. Once passed, it cannot be recovered or renewed. Therefore, every moment should be valued and lived with intention. How we choose to use our time reflects what we value most in life. Time spent with family and friends is priceless, strengthening relationships and enriching our lives with meaningful memories and experiences. Whether it's a family dinner, a walk with a friend, or a simple conversation, these interactions bring joy and meaning to our lives. Also, self-time is vital, allowing us to reconnect with our inner self and recharge our emotional and mental batteries. Time spent in self-reflection and self-care is essential for maintaining mental health and personal development.

In addition, time allocated for work and professional achievements is also important. However, balance is key. It is essential to find a balance between work and personal life so that we do not get lost in one dimension of our existence.

An often overlooked aspect of time is its ability to enable us to contribute to the good of others and society. Whether it's volunteering, helping someone, or participating in community activities, our time can be a powerful force for positive change and social impact. To make the most of our time, it's important to practice mindfulness and be present in every moment. This means living consciously and appreciating the present moment, without being constantly distracted by the past or worried about the future. Time is one of life's most valuable gifts. Through its wise use and balancing various aspects of our existence, we can live a more fulfilling and balanced life. Time gives us the opportunity to live, love, learn and grow.

It is our responsibility to use it in ways that not only enrich our own lives, but also contribute to the good of those around us. Physical health allows us to enjoy life in all its forms. From simple activities, such as walks in the park, to more dynamic experiences, such as traveling or sports, a healthy body is a vehicle that allows us to explore and enjoy the world. A balanced diet, regular exercise and adequate rest are key elements in maintaining optimal physical health. Mental health is just as important and often less discussed. In the modern world, where stress and anxiety are increasingly present, taking care of mental health is crucial. Activities such as meditation, yoga, spending time in nature, or simply moments of relaxation and tranquility can contribute significantly to mental and emotional well-being.

In addition, interpersonal relationships play an important role in our mental health. The emotional and social support we receive from our family and friends can have a profound impact on our well-being. A sense of belonging, love, understanding, and connection to others are essential for robust mental health. It's also important to recognize the warning signs of health problems and seek professional help when needed. Our health should never be neglected or taken as a guarantee. Prevention, early recognition and appropriate treatment of health problems are crucial to maintain an optimal quality of life. Health is a priceless gift that allows us to live life to the fullest. By maintaining robust physical and mental health, we ensure that we can take advantage of all the opportunities and joys that life has to offer. It is our responsibility to take care of this gift, to value it and to protect it. Health is the foundation on which every aspect of our lives is built, and therefore deserves all our effort and attention.

In a society that often glorifies hard work and professional success, it can be easy to fall into the trap of letting careers dominate all aspects of our lives. However, excessive dedication to work can lead to burnout, stress, and neglect of other important areas of life, such as health, relationships, and personal development. Work-life balance involves recognizing that while work is an important part of our lives, it shouldn't be our only focus. It is essential to set aside time for ourselves, our hobbies and interests, to relax and recharge our batteries. This includes spending quality time with family and friends, practicing activities that bring us joy and satisfaction, and taking care of our physical and mental health. At the same time, maintaining a satisfactory level of commitment and professional performance is important. Balance does not mean neglecting professional responsibilities, but finding a way to excel in your career without sacrificing other aspects of life.

This can be achieved by setting healthy boundaries, managing time effectively, and prioritizing tasks. In addition, it is important to recognize that work-life balance does not mean the same thing to everyone and can vary throughout life. Different career stages and changes in personal life may require adjustments in how we manage time and resources. An essential aspect of maintaining this balance is to be aware of our own health and well-being. It's important to watch out for signs of stress or burnout and take steps to protect our mental and physical health.

This may include asking for help when needed and making sure we have time to rest and relax. Work-life balance is crucial for a healthy and fulfilling life. This balance allows us to enjoy professional successes while maintaining our health, relationships and personal happiness. By constantly being aware and adjusting how we divide time and energy between different aspects of life, we can live in harmony and with a sense of total fulfillment.

About the desire for wealth and to consider true success

The desire to develop and achieve superior material comfort is a natural and powerful trait in each of us. It inspires us to work, learn and develop in all aspects of our lives, making our lives successful. In the pursuit of success and satisfaction, we are often motivated by this inner desire to reach new heights. However, it is vital to recognize that this desire can turn into a compulsive force, which can distort our perspectives and pull us away from core values. When she becomes obsessive, her desire for wealth can lead to neglecting meaningful aspects of life, such as relationships with others and appreciating their efforts. It is essential to pay attention to our relationships.

A vital aspect of a balanced life is to balance the desire for material progress with the appreciation of people and their work. This balance helps us maintain close ties with those around us and reminds us that success should not come at the expense of others or neglect their efforts. To be successful, we need to focus on our efforts.

We must remember that success is not an individual race to material prosperity. Valuing others and their influences on civilization is essential to a truly fulfilling life. Considering and recognizing the efforts of others can enrich us in ways that cannot be measured in economic terms.

The aspiration to develop and attain a higher level of material comfort is an integral and significant part of our human nature. However, we must be aware of the risk of this desire becoming excessive and ensure that we remain true to our core values. A solid balance between the desire for material achievements and responsibility towards others and their work can give us a life full of meaning and achievement.

It is crucial not to seek personal enrichment at the expense of others or to pursue goals at all costs, ignoring the well-being of others. Authentic achievement is not measured by the accumulation of wealth or by the impression we make on others, but by respectable achievements and contribution to the common good.

In a world where material value is often considered of paramount importance, it is essential to remember that success is not just about wealth and social status. Authentic realization is a broader and complex concept that goes beyond these material aspects. Although material wealth can bring comfort, it does not guarantee happiness or personal satisfaction.

Many societies conclude that material success has not brought them long-term satisfaction or fulfillment. This demonstrates that success cannot be defined solely in terms of financial or social status, but involves a wider range of elements. Health, happiness, relationships, and personal development are just as important, if not more essential, to evaluating our real success.

Another important dimension is the impact we have on those around us and on the world around us. Achievement should not be selfish or limited to personal benefit, but should include a positive impact on the common good. Selfless actions, generosity, and service to others can bring deep satisfaction and add significant value to our lives.

We should not limit ourselves to self-improvement, but seek achievement that encompasses a variety of aspects, including physical health, happiness, relationships, and personal development. True prosperity comes from satisfaction found in good deeds and contributing to the happiness of others. Thus, the realization becomes much deeper and more satisfying, bringing benefits both for ourselves and for society at large.

Frequently, we are encouraged to compare ourselves to others and strive to achieve social standards. However, we must recognize that happiness and success are subjective and can vary significantly from person to person. What works for one individual is not necessarily applicable to another. The truth is that each of us has our own definition of happiness and success, and these definitions can include different aspects of life, such as health, family, relationships, passions or community involvement.

Societal pressure to adopt conventional norms and values can often be overwhelming. However, it is essential to remember that these values do not have to be universally valid for every individual. What matters most is what brings us true happiness and satisfaction, which can vary significantly from person to person and change over the course of a lifetime.

Happiness and success can come from various aspects of our lives. For some, physical health and well-being may be a priority, while for others, relationships and personal connections can be of paramount importance. Some may find self-realization in their passions and interests, while others may find their involvement in the community most rewarding.

It is essential to recognize and value the diversity of definitions of happiness and success. There is no universal formula for a happy life or achieving success. Everyone has the right to define and follow their own path that aligns with their unique values, goals, and personal circumstances.

We need to release the pressure to follow societal norms and encourage diversity in pursuit of happiness and success. By creating a more empathetic and diverse society, considering different interpretations of these concepts, and encouraging others to pursue their own goals, we can build a richer and more satisfying world for all.

It is unbearable to disregard the simple and respected things in our lives, such as our physical condition, family, friends, our joining with the environment and our precious time. The usual desire to improve, and development is normal and engaging. However, we must carry it out knowingly and responsibly so as not to lose the vision of the right spirit of life.

Properly defined, achievement should not be limited to tax amounts, but contain various characteristics such as gaiety, private gratification, and a progressive involvement in civilization. The real treasure is found when we pay attention to what matters and live in the current with gratitude and understanding. It is an achievement that brings reliable satisfaction and that donates to an improved world for all.

The power of visualization and energy transformation

In my journey to recover from gambling addiction and bookmarking, and in the procedure of writing this book, I learned that to help you honestly; You have to appreciate and practice imagining. Meditation is a dominant method that allows you to venture your thoughts and goals into a perceptible form, see them in the eye of attention and feel them in your heart. It is a tool that can fundamentally change the way you approach life and help you overcome gambling addiction.

When I was caught up in the whirlwind of gambling, I was inclined to sharpen my harmful energy. I felt embarrassed, dissatisfied, and dissatisfied at every step of my life. I lost confidence in myself, and this negative energy seemed to pull me deeper into the depths of my addiction. However, when I started learning about meditation, I learned how to convert this bad energy into something good and productive.

Imagine that every moment of defeat, every suffering, and every mistake in the past is like a brick in a building. This building is your life, and you are the main builder. Every time you felt anger, guilt, or guilt because of gambling, you added a brick to this build. But now comes the enchanted part - you can begin to turn these opposite bricks into positive bricks.

Imagine every bad brick as a building block. In your mind, start painting with bright colors and convert them into optimistic bricks. Every past mistake can become a valuable lesson, every moment of weakness can become a source of strength, and every moment of guilt can become an opportunity for forgiveness and growth.

Changing a bad unit into a somewhat decent one helps recover command and control over your life. But the imagination doesn't stop there. You can also visualize what you are about to do with cheerfulness and confidence. Instead of putting yourself at risk in gambling, you can visualize danger and desire dedicated to your industry.

In your attention, you can see every step you take towards achievement in your business. You can feel adrenaline and satisfaction when you succeed in entrepreneurship. Meditation can become a continuous foundation of motivation and inspiration, forcing you to overcome any obstacle and turn your imagination into reality.

So to help you with this book, you have to imagine. Learn to turn bad energy into something good and build your own life the way you want. Instead of taking risks in gambling, take risks in business, where your efforts can bring tangible rewards and grow your life. Visualize your future; Believe physically and in your power to change. Overcome addiction and build a meaningful and fulfilling life. It's time to be the master of your destiny.

Turning Poverty into Power: Turning Lack into Opportunity

"I was never poor enough to become rich enough." Ciprian Ipate

The poor often possess an invaluable resource that can give them a unique chance to become rich, the same resource that has been the driving force behind many success stories: flexibility. Yes, resilience and determination to overcome poverty can be powerful engines of personal growth and prosperity.

When discussing poverty and wealth, many focus on one's financial resources or social conditions. However, failure does not have to be a permanent sentence; Alternatively, it can be your starting step to persistent struggle and continued growth. Wealth is not incomplete to tax resources, but can also contain a wealth of knowledge, relationships with family and friends, and donations to the public.

In search of the inspiring story of "Andrew Carnegie".

Who grew up in a very poor family in Scotland, but settled in the United States at an early age. During his lifetime, he explored the many ways to manage scarcity and turn it into an event. Through his efforts and knowledge, Carnegie became one of the richest men in the world in the nineteenth century and frequently funded public libraries and educational institutions to give others the chance to improve their standard of living just as he did.

Another remarkable story is that of Howard Schultz, creator of Starbucks. He, too, grew up in an underprivileged family in Brooklyn, New York, and faced an uphill battle to pursue his thoughts, imagination and dreams. Schultz explores many ways to educate himself, become a successful professional leader, and transform his small café into an international kingdom. This is a clear demonstration that early poverty can be a foundation of strength and inspiration.

In a similar way, let's see the example of Oprah Winfrey, who grew up in a low-income family in Mississippi and went through very problematic and difficult youth experiences. However, she used her information and hard work and exploited these involvements to become one of the most influential and wealthy women in the world. Oprah is an amazing example of how initial poverty can facilitate success and how we can overcome difficulties in poverty with willpower and perseverance.

These examples teach us that initial poverty can be a source of motivation and a significant factor in making smart decisions. Instead of running away from poverty, try to learn and take lessons from it and use its limited properties to mature and achieve your goals. Anyone can start from scratch and build a practical life if they have passion, self-confidence and determination.

It's like being prepared for anything; It's like exercising to make your body solid and well-prepared to carry out your daily activities with energy rather than laziness. Visualizing is like imagining you succeeded; If you've been successful in the past, you can recall that success, and that will motivate you. It is like awakening your spiritual powers. It is scientifically proven that self-imagining affects the body because it is directly related to our nervous system, which stimulates emotions. Through visualization, you can trigger your desires. It gives you confidence, reduces stress, boosts motivation and improves performance.

The basics of entrepreneurship and gambling

In the world of entrepreneurship, lessons learned from gambling can pave the way to success. Experienced gamblers bring unique skills gained through their experience to the business field. These individuals enjoy significant advantages, the main one being the ability to make quick decisions and assess risks strategically. Such skills are invaluable for an entrepreneur, giving them the opportunity to use valuable knowledge gained from both inside and outside the gaming world to sculpt their success into entrepreneurship.

Entrepreneurship involves creating and managing a business with the aim of generating profit, requiring a revolutionary approach and deliberate risk-taking. In gambling, every bet is made with the unique hope of winning. Like this desire for business success, I am on a journey of exploration, diving deeper into areas such as risk, strategic thinking, and game theory, which are fundamental to success in the business world. I discover a path to achievement, woven from the complexity and uncertainty of gambling.

Through interviews with entrepreneurs who navigated successes and failures, turning risks into triumphs, their story becomes a transformative odyssey. It emphasizes that failure is not an obstacle, but an essential element in building a successful entrepreneurial career.

The interaction between risk and reward

The interaction between risk and reward plays a key role in the assessment process. The prospects for higher returns are often accompanied by an increased level of risk. Finding the right balance between these two aspects depends on factors such as the magnitude of the risk, specific objectives and the context of the assessment.

Striking a balance between risk-taking and reaping rewards is crucial in both the business world and gambling. Approaching a business project has much in common with participating in an exciting game, reflecting the fundamental principles of gambling. We explore how to navigate between calculated risk-taking and maximizing rewards, both in business and gambling.

Imagine this situation: when you launch a business or participate in a game, there is a level of uncertainty, a lack of predictability. Taking risks involves trying strategies that may not always yield the desired results, although in case of success, considerable advantages can be obtained, such as growth resulting from one's entrepreneurial activities.

Empathetic involvement of risk hunger when initiating new business projects. The concept of "risk appetite" measures a person's comfort level in taking bold chances. Some prefer to take risks, while others opt for safety and engage in less risky projects. Risk implies the chance that an unfortunate event will happen or not. It's part of every business, so it's important not to be afraid to take calculated risks.

Exploring the right balance between risk and reward requires a careful approach, taking into account individual circumstances, objectives and specifics of the enterprise. This is like a guide to help you understand the nature of risks and how to manage them throughout your journey. Entrepreneurial.

During starting a new business, it is essential to consider both risks and profits. Some entrepreneurs take an aggressive approach, while others are more conservative. There are high-risk businesses such as financial services, casinos and gambling, and cryptocurrency trading; in these areas, entrepreneurs take high risks and can also achieve proportional returns, since the risk and reward are directly proportional; The greater the risk, the greater the potential reward, and vice versa. For example, purchasing a cryptocurrency and facing a massive loss of investment due to legal issues shows how volatile this sector can be.

On the other hand, if the value of that cryptocurrency increases, the profit will be significant and the return on investment will exceed that of other businesses. A conservative entrepreneur who avoids high risks will opt for low-risk businesses, such as retail or online, where risk and reward are moderate but competition can also be intense.

ITS is a complex field that explores how people make choices. It includes reasoning, emotions and external factors. Cognitive biases, heuristics, risk awareness, and emotional influences are key. Understanding them helps us understand why decisions aren't always optimal.

In gambling, quick decision making under pressure is essential; These skills are valuable in business as well. Playing a game like stone-paper-scissors, where you need to make quick decisions, also applies to business. For example, running a lemonade store on sunny days requires quick decisions to meet increased demand, demonstrating the importance of adaptability and quick business thinking.

Using intuition and analysis in vital business-related decisions, learning from the principles of entrepreneurship drawn from gambling, involves trusting instinct and making situation-based decisions. Similar to gambling, where the situation is constantly changing and nothing goes according to plan, we must conclude according to uncertain conditions. By combining intuition with analysis, we need to find the optimal balance between feeling and rational thinking to make the most advantageous choices for business success. By comparing these fundamentals, we can better understand the decision-making process, recognizing the importance of perceptual, emotional, and situational factors.

Managing a gambling bankroll and business cash flow highlights the critical importance of managing finances. Business, similar to participating in a game, requires prudent management of financial resources. For example, in poker, it is essential to be aware of how much you spend on each hand in order to keep playing.
Similarly, in business, effective management of cash inflows and outflows is key to success. For example, in a burger shop, it is crucial to secure enough funds to purchase the necessary ingredients, the equivalent of bankroll management in gambling. Therefore, this section links financial management in games and business, emphasizing the importance of wise financial choices.

Budgeting techniques and financial forecasts

This section addresses effective ways to organize finances and anticipate the financial situation. Budget planning and financial projections are comparable to preparing a party, where you need to estimate costs and allocate resources wisely. In business, budgeting involves allocating funds to different segments, such as consumables or advertising, and financial projection helps estimate future income or expenses.
It is essential to draw up a complete business plan that ensures the smooth running of the business. Careful planning and financial forecasts are like preparing for a party, anticipating the number of guests and the amount of food needed. Using smart methods for managing budget and making financial forecasts, we ensure that our business is on the right track.

The application of game theory to business strategy is a sophisticated method of navigating the complex competitive landscape of the modern market. We analyze in detail how the principles of game theory can be used not only in direct interactions with competitors, but also in strategic planning, negotiations and internal business development.

Considering game theory as a framework for making smart and deliberate business moves, in-game strategies, where every move is calculated to maximize the chances of winning, are reflected in the business world, where every decision and action can have significant implications.

For example, in the marketing of cakes, the emergence of a new competitor in the market can be considered a strategic challenge. Using game theory principles, you can anticipate competitor movements and formulate responses that maintain your competitive edge, such as diversifying your product range or implementing innovative marketing strategies.

Integrating gamified elements into corporate policy can transform employee skills, teamwork, and problem-solving. Gamified training programs, simulations and team-building activities with game elements make the learning process more attractive and stimulate a positive corporate culture. The aim is to create a dynamic and innovative work environment where efficiency and creativity are encouraged, using technologies such as virtual reality and augmented reality for immersive learning experiences, while traditional games promote strategic thinking and collaboration.

Exploring how strategies in gambling can inspire innovation in the business model is another valuable application of game theory. By observing ingenious tactics used by players to win, businesses can discover new ways to adapt and thrive. This

can mean monitoring market trends and adapting supply to meet changing consumer needs.
For example, an online store that observes ingenious strategies applied by players may adopt innovative approaches in the business, such as creating special packages or loyalty programs to attract and retain customers. Thus, ideas inspired by games can turn into effective business strategies, stimulating the continuous growth and development of the company.

In conclusion, integrating game theory into business strategy requires strategic thinking, innovation and adaptability. Through this approach, businesses can improve market interactions and competition, as well as internal culture, motivating employees to think strategically and collaborate effectively. Game theory provides the tools to successfully navigate a dynamic business environment, turning challenges into opportunities and stimulating constant growth and innovation.

Learning from Mistakes

Learning from mistakes, or failures, is a valuable and fundamental process in personal and professional development. It involves detailed analysis of errors and obstacles to improve future skills and strategies. The process requires identifying what went wrong, understanding the factors that contributed to those failures, applying the knowledge gained, and implementing corrective measures. Adopting an attitude of growth and viewing failures as valuable learning opportunities can lead to remarkable transformations in both career and personal life.

For example, in the context of entrepreneurship, turning losses or failures into valuable lessons is crucial to business growth. Let's take the case of gambling: if you lose a game, instead of being overwhelmed by disappointment, you can use this experience as an opportunity to learn more effective strategies for the future. This principle is also applicable in business. For example, a bakery owner experiencing declining sales may choose to innovate by testing new recipes or diversifying their offering to attract a broader customer base.

Another example could be an entrepreneur who runs an online store of handmade products. If they initially don't get significant sales, they might decide to place their products on more visible online platforms by offering detailed descriptions, attractive photos, and demo videos. This change in strategy could lead to a significant increase in sales. Thus, initial failures become opportunities to learn how to improve marketing strategies and product presentation.

It is also crucial to develop a corporate culture that encourages innovation and calculated risk-taking. Creating a work environment where each team member is stimulated to bring new ideas and take well-thought-out risks can be a key factor in the success of a business. For example, in an office where brainstorming creative ideas is common practice, it creates an atmosphere conducive to business success. It not only stimulates innovation, but also encourages smart risk-taking after careful consideration.

A concrete example can be a designer working in a technology products company. In such an environment that values innovation, the designer could propose a new feature for a product and, if it is well received, be rewarded accordingly. This creates a culture in which risk-taking is accepted and encouraged, as long as it is preceded by rigorous analysis and strategic planning.

In conclusion, learning from mistakes and turning failures into opportunities for growth are essential elements at both an individual and corporate level. This process is comparable to playing a strategic game, where every move is well thought out and oriented towards continuous improvement and long-term success. Smart risk-taking, innovation and adaptability are the pillars that support growth and development in any field, turning obstacles into opportunities for expansion and improvement.

Computable vs. Reckless Risks

Computable business risk is one that can be assessed or predicted by using historical data, mathematical models, or other analytical methods. These risks, based on known variables, allow for a degree of foresight and are essential for strategic planning and informed decision-making in business and finance. For example, a company can assess the risk of investing in new technologies or launching a new product on the market based on rigorous market research and financial analysis.

Reckless risk, on the other hand, involves actions taken without proper assessment of possible consequences or detailed investigation. This type of risk is often impulsive and lacks careful consideration, and can lead to serious consequences. For example, a company that decides to expand rapidly into a new market without understanding the local culture or market requirements may suffer significant financial losses and reputational damage.

Differentiating between smart risks and reckless choices is crucial in entrepreneurship. It is important to make carefully evaluated choices, distinguishing between taking calculated risks and making hasty decisions. In business, market analysis and assessment of competition before launching a new product are examples of calculable risks, while impulsive decisions, such as changing prices without proper market analysis, are reckless risks.

Adopting a strategic approach requires establishing a framework for assessing risks and opportunities. Developing a system for risk recognition and assessment is essential, as is a handmade jewelry retailer deciding whether launching a new product line is a profitable opportunity or a major risk.

It is vital to recognize that not all risks can be anticipated or avoided. There is always the possibility of unexpected losses or problems. Preparation and planning for such eventualities, such as securing financial resources to minimize negative impacts, demonstrates prudent management of calculable risks.

In conclusion, distinguishing between calculable and reckless risks is fundamental in effectively managing a business. Computable risk facilitates strategic planning and intelligence-driven decisions, while avoiding reckless risks protects the business from potentially devastating effects. Being a successful entrepreneur means skillfully navigating between these types of risks, making smart choices that promote business growth while minimizing exposure to impulsive and uninformed decisions. It is a balanced strategy, where every decision is well weighted and supported by detailed analyses, thus ensuring the success and sustainability of the business in a dynamic business environment.

The transition from player to creator is an essential transformation process that allows us to move from passive consumers to active content producers. This metamorphosis begins with recognizing one's passions and talents and choosing a resourceful direction – whether it's game development, writing, art, or any other creative field. It is crucial to learn the necessary skills in depth, whether through online resources or traditional courses. This journey involves seeing failure as a learning tool, essential for continuous improvement. Perseverance and dedication are imperative to improve skills and succeed in the desired transformation.

Changing the mindset from luck addiction to taking control is a fundamental step in this transformation. Let's say we're in a game where luck plays a major role. The transition from player to creator is equivalent to going from hoping for luck to taking initiative and making things happen. For example, in running a gardening business, it's up to luck to rely on the perfect weather. But as a creator, you start using proactive techniques, such as researching the best planting times or using optimal topsoil, to influence your garden's growth. It's about moving from letting things happen to random to being the strategist shaping outcomes in your business.

Developing a proactive attitude, instead of a reactive one, is vital to success. Adopting a proactive mindset, where you take initiative instead of just reacting to circumstances, means you have total control, prepare and act before things reveal themselves. An example can be a small online store selling handcrafted products. With a proactive approach, it could plan effective marketing campaigns in advance and create festive products well ahead of season.

On the other hand, a reactive approach would mean waiting until the last minute and reacting to circumstances as they arise. It's like playing a game where you're always behind, trying to catch up. An emerging mindset is one where you are proactive and make things happen before they happen, instead of being reactive and responding to situations after they have already happened. It's like playing a game where you're constantly one step ahead, making business decisions strategically and predictively.

Adaptability and flexibility

Adaptability, the talent to regulate and thrive in changing conditions, involves openness to new ideas and effective responses to unforeseen situations. Flexibility, on the other hand, is the ability to effortlessly adjust in the face of change, while remaining agile and responsive. In different environments, flexibility can mean openness to different perspectives, multifunctional skills, or a willingness to help and collaborate. Combined, adaptability and flexibility are essential characteristics that allow individuals to navigate uncertainties and remain resilient in the face of challenges.

We learn from various fields, from the ever-changing dynamics of gambling to strategic business pivots. We examine how we can extract awareness from the constant changes in gaming and apply these lessons to adjust our business strategy. In the gaming industry, the scene is changing rapidly, which requires an adaptable and agile approach. Similarly, in commerce, flexibility means being prepared to adapt your method when conditions require it. Taking the example of a small clothing store, flexibility can mean quickly changing inventory to align with the latest fashion styles, adjusting your stock to meet customer demands. Essentially, it's about altering your business game plan to stay competitive in the market.

The importance of adapting to changes in the market and customer behaviour is crucial. Case studies are essential tools to understand and adapt to these changes. For example, considering a bookstore, if you notice a shift towards online shopping and ebooks, adapting your approach could mean offering a wider selection of digital books on your website. Such adjustments keep you up with customer preferences and market trends.

Cases and case studies provide valuable lessons based on real-world experiences of other companies that have successfully navigated market changes. From innovative marketing strategies to adjusting product range, these stories are like a playbook filled with exciting tactics based on the achievements and challenges of others. We learn how to adapt our business to market fluctuations and consumer behavior, turning these changes into opportunities.

Adaptability and flexibility in business are not only about responding to change, but also about anticipating and driving those changes. This involves a deep understanding of the industry, a clear vision of the future, and the ability to innovate and experiment. From adopting new technologies to exploring new markets, adaptability and flexibility are fundamental to staying relevant and thriving in an ever-evolving business environment.

Explore the fascinating journeys of successful entrepreneurs through a series of engaging and easy-to-follow interviews. These business pioneers share their stories, providing exclusive access to their business initiation and development experiences. In these dialogues, you will discover the source of their inspiration, the origin of innovative business ideas, and learn about the effective and personalized leadership styles that led them to success.

This series of conversations also gives us lessons learned from failures, providing real, authentic insight into how to turn mistakes into valuable lessons. Each interview is an inspiration to bring innovation to your own business and offers practical advice on how to balance work with personal life. New entrepreneurs will find in these stories invaluable tips that will help them navigate the challenges of start-ups and build successful businesses.

Plus, you'll have the opportunity to learn from business owners who turned challenges into triumphs. Imagine being able to extract valuable lessons from a bakery owner who was able to turn customer scarcity into a steady stream of business through creative and innovative approaches. Each story is a source of information and motivation, coming directly from those who have gone through similar experiences.

But these discussions are not just simple interviews; They represent a unique chance to learn directly from experts who have understood and mastered the art of business. You'll gain practical wisdom, be captivated by their success stories, and discover strategies and approaches that have turned challenges into opportunities. Get inspired by these conversations and get ready to write your own entrepreneurial story.

In this extended series, you'll meet entrepreneurs who have succeeded in fields ranging from technology to services, and from commerce to the creative industry. Each interview brings to the fore a new aspect of the business, whether it is marketing, finance, innovation or developing organizational culture. You'll have access to experiences ranging from startups to large corporations, giving you a wide range of perspectives and strategies.

These conversations are more than just business lessons; They are life stories that talk about resilience, adaptability and the courage to dream big. Each story is a testament to entrepreneurship and inspiration for anyone who wants to pursue their dream of becoming a successful entrepreneur.

Analysis of successes and failures

Case studies illustrate how risk-taking in business can lead to either remarkable triumphs or unexpected setbacks. Exploring companies' real stories allows us to see how their risk decisions have materialized, whether in triumphs or challenges. For example, a small tech company that decides to launch a new product could either drive the company's progress with formidable success or face complications if the product doesn't meet expectations.

On the other hand, analyzing a failed product and its impact on the company can provide valuable insights into effective policies and risky strategies. Uncovering the authentic stories of companies, exploring the risks taken and analyzing their consequences gives us valuable insight into business challenges and triumphs.
The lessons drawn from the practical experiences of other entrepreneurs are invaluable. Understanding in detail what worked and what didn't work in their experiences adds immense value to our own initiatives. Imagine reading a book that, towards the end, reveals insights gathered from interactions with numerous business people. These lessons can range from tackling challenges to achieve success to navigating business difficulties.

In the complicated dance of life, success and failure are partners waltzing through the narrative of our journey. These are not abstract concepts, but integral parts of personal and professional growth. Exploring the nuances of success and failure, the criteria for evaluating them, and the importance of failure analysis is essential.
Success and failure are inherent aspects of any business, each with its own unique challenges.

For some, success can mean financial achievements or achieving personal goals, while for others, it can be about positively influencing society. Failure, often seen as the

opposite of success, is a vital milestone on the road to learning and development.
Success and failure follow a universal truth: the importance of continuous and intelligent work. In the business world, success can be measured by increased revenue, customer satisfaction, or market share, while failure can provide a chance to reevaluate and learn, redirecting efforts toward a more efficient path.

Failure analysis is not about assigning blame, but about understanding why things didn't go according to plan and using this information as a learning resource. This includes identifying the problems that led to failure, assessing their impact, and developing strategies to prevent their recurrence in the future.
Examining failures effectively requires identifying the root causes and understanding the events that led to undesirable outcomes. Recognising these aspects is crucial for continuous adaptation and improvement. Ultimately, adaptability and the ability to learn from failures are essential to long-term success.

Analysis of successes and failures is not a singular task, but a continuous process of development. Deep understanding of the relationship between success and failure allows us to navigate life's journey with flexibility and adaptability, promising uninterrupted progress.

Action Plan

For those who aspire to total control and want to shift their focus to entrepreneurship, this applied guide is designed to turn risks into opportunities. Assuming failure is not an obstacle, but a necessary step to get closer to success. In the entrepreneurial world, failures are viewed as vital learning opportunities.

Redefining failure is crucial. Instead of seeing it as an end, we need to see it as a turning point, a moment of recalibration in a better direction. Historically, failures have often led to significant progress and remarkable achievements. A bankruptcy is not the end of the road, but the basis on which future success is built.

The inspiring stories of entrepreneurs who experienced insolvency and came back stronger than before are living proof of this reality. Psychologically, how an entrepreneur manages bankruptcy is decisive for the future of his business. By adopting the "phoenix" mentality, we learn to rise from our ashes and relaunch our business with new forces.

Plans to reinvent and restart your business after failure are vital. These involve preparing to increase resilience and developing a solution-oriented mindset. Recognizing and harnessing the lessons hidden in every failure is essential to progress.
Using negative feedback and losses to build a more robust business model can position us for long-term success.

It is also crucial to maintain inspiration and remain dedicated, even in the face of difficulties. Methods of managing stress and keeping a healthy outlook are essential; With a smart pivot, we must decide when to persist and when to change path.
Identifying the right time to make critical strategic changes can be a decisive factor in the success of a business. Case studies of famous pivots after failure and incorporating failures into corporate culture are valuable examples of learning.

Creating a culture where the team learns from mistakes and continually improves is crucial. Great leaders turn failures into learning opportunities for their teams, helping them understand how to avoid repeating similar mistakes.
Systems and procedures for assessing what is incorrect and how to avoid repeating it are also valuable tools. This includes feedback and post-mortem investigations for failed projects and business plans.

In conclusion, solid steps to get up after a significant insolvency or failure, tactical planning and setting realistic goals for the new stage of business are fundamental. Always consider failure as the keystone of success and revise key concepts to reinforce the message that failure is a predecessor to success. Motivation and inspiration are the keys to achieving a successful ending.

Summary

My book explores the reflective journey of transformation from spectator to active participant, navigating the territories of gaming and entrepreneurship. I shared my personal journey into gambling addiction, experiencing various stages such as seduction, challenges, relapses, pandemic disruptions, therapy and group support. I struggle with addiction through its ups and downs, highlighting the ongoing nature of healing and the power of shared experiences.

We have highlighted effective methods and ways to quit gambling, personally testing a large part of them. In the book, I tried to emphasize the shift from a chance addiction to a prudent exercise of influence, encouraging a proactive mindset and favoring flexibility. Drawing a parallel between the complexity of gambling dynamics and the obstacles in entrepreneurship, the book emphasizes the continuous need for learning.

It is a continuous cycle of development and adaptability, essential for achieving a balance between risk-taking and prudence, knowing the interdependence between success and failure in business and life. The actionable roadmap provides guidelines for the entrepreneurial journey, providing insights into redefining failure, constructively navigating bankruptcy, and turning failures into opportunities for growth and development. The emphasis is on motivation, encouragement, and cultivating a culture that draws lessons from missteps.

I won the war against gambling addiction through resilience and determination, which paved the way for an entrepreneurial journey that defined my success. I hope my book will serve as a comprehensive compass for those struggling with gambling addiction and navigating to success in entrepreneurship.

Recognition

I want to thank from the bottom of my heart all those who have been by my side in the most difficult moments of my life. Your trust and unshakable support have been invaluable to me. Special recognition goes to my family and, in particular, to my children. You were my beacon of hope, teaching me the valuable lesson of finding reasons to smile, even on the most difficult days or when life seemed to be most daunting.

I am also extremely grateful to my mentors, colleagues and friends who have been instrumental in my entrepreneurial journey. The guidance, encouragement and knowledge shared by you have been essential to navigate the complexities of entrepreneurship, contributing significantly to my personal and professional growth.
In the spirit of self-knowledge and appreciation, I also want to take a moment to thank myself,

echoing the encouraging words of Snoop Dogg:

"I want to thank myself for doing all this hard work. I want to thank myself for not having days off. I want to thank myself for never giving up. I want to thank myself for always being a giver and trying to give more than I received. I want to thank myself for trying to do more good than harm. I want to thank myself for always being me at all times."

This journey of recovery, growth and entrepreneurship has been as challenging as it has been rewarding, and it is a path we have traveled with the support of many. For that, I am eternally grateful.

"You'll never change your life until you change something you do every day. The secret to your success lies in your daily routine." - John C. Maxwell

Printed in Great Britain
by Amazon

39876953R00118